LIFE IN YELLOW

LIFE IN YELLOW

A MEMOIR

LIZ IRONS

NEW DEGREE PRESS

COPYRIGHT © 2021 LIZ IRONS

LIFE IN YELLOW

A Memoir

ISBN   978-1-63676-877-9 *Paperback*

978-1-63676-878-6 *Kindle Ebook*

978-1-63676-879-3 *Ebook*

To my mother and grandmother, thank you for showing me how to raise my voice, trust in my heart, and eat copious amounts of Italian food. Thanks to you, I know how to let the light in.

CONTENTS

PART 1.	**CANCER**	**11**
CHAPTER 1.	AUGUST	13
CHAPTER 2.	A SONG IN TWO PARTS	21
CHAPTER 3.	DEER	31
CHAPTER 4.	ENGLISH	35
CHAPTER 5.	YELLOW SOCKS	41
CHAPTER 6.	ICE	49
CHAPTER 7.	DC STATEHOOD	53
CHAPTER 8.	TESORO	61
PART 2.	**COUNTRIES**	**69**
CHAPTER 9.	THE FIRST WAR OF ITALIAN INDEPENDENCE	71
CHAPTER 10.	YOU, ME, SICILY	81
CHAPTER 11.	HALLOWEEN NIGHT	89
CHAPTER 12.	TEN P.M. IN PARIS	95
CHAPTER 13.	ROMA CITTÀ APERTA	101
CHAPTER 14.	LISBON	111

PART 3.   **CLOSURE**   **119**

CHAPTER 15.   GEMMA   121

CHAPTER 16.   HOCKEY   125

CHAPTER 17.   N.E.D. = NO EVIDENCE OF DISEASE   131

CHAPTER 18.   AUGUST II   137

CHAPTER 19.   WIND   141

              ACKNOWLEDGEMENTS   145

              APPENDIX   149

"*The act was an exorcism of relief for Florentino Ariza, for when he put the violin back into its case and walked down the dead streets without looking back, he no longer felt that he was leaving the next morning but that he had gone away many years before with the irrevocable determination never to return.*"

GABRIEL GARCÍA MÁRQUEZ,
LOVE IN THE TIME OF CHOLERA

PART 1

CANCER

CHAPTER 1

AUGUST

———

I had come to associate death with the month of August, which is ironically the month that I was born. It was now the third August that someone in our family had died, a fact that stuck like peanut butter between my teeth and produced a slight, ringing noise deep within my ears. In August of 2014, it was the sudden and untimely death of my father.

I was about to turn fifteen years old.

The afternoon I learned of my father's death, I walked around my small town of Newtown, Pennsylvania with my friend Mary Kate. Together, the two of us devoured soft pretzels and milkshakes sold to us by the Pennsylvania Dutch at a nearby farmer's market.

"What kind of milkshakes should we get?" she asked me.

"Maybe strawberry?" I sheepishly suggested.

Years later, I am still baffled by my mind's ability to imprint the smallest details surrounding that day and how strange it is that all of this time later, I still know the exact table where we sat that late afternoon.

After we finished our soft pretzels and milkshakes, the two of us slowly walked back home together. Her neighborhood was just across the street from mine.

I walked in the front door to find my mother sitting at our dining room table, head in her hands. She looked up at me, eyes heavy with the kind of exhaustion that only comes from knowing too much.

"Sit down next to me," she said, pointing to the dining room chair next to her. The consoling tone of her voice took me by surprise.

It felt as though the world around me had suddenly shifted, as the strawberry milkshake smile slowly melted off my face and was quickly replaced with a newfound sense of fear.

"What is it? What happened?" I asked.

And then—in an instant—my mother told me.

"Your father passed away last night. Your grandparents just called to tell me."

Pain lingered in the soft edges of my mother's voice.

Pain took a moment to reach me, but within an instant, settled right in my gut.

My father was dead. My knees buckled and I fell to our dining room floor.

~

At this point, I hadn't physically seen my father in over seven years.

Our very last meeting had been the afternoon of my First Holy Communion, in a quick minute or two encounter that is now frozen in the back of my mind. It was May 12, 2007. I realize now as I write this, that today is the 14th anniversary of that day. I don't know how I feel, or if I truly feel anything about the date at all.

Yet, fourteen years ago, there I stood: White communion dress. Soft brown hair curled with an expectant smile that lit up the rest of my face. And there he was, looming over me, bearing a wide and toothy smile, the same eyes reflected back at me from above. For years after, I hated having his eyes.

But that afternoon, at seven years old, I was a small cherub of grace and reverent Catholicism.

My father stopped to say hello for just a few moments before disappearing back into his red Chevy pickup truck. I don't remember what words we exchanged, what he was wearing, or how I felt at the time.

I didn't know then that I would never see him alive again.

~

Daniel Irons was about average height, heavy set, brunette with a perennially rosy face and a mischievous boy's smile. As a child, it often felt like he was a kid too. For the few years leading up to that final meeting, I had been carted back and forth to my father's house every other weekend. Such as the case with many children of divorce, my father wanted to be my friend.

He wanted me to like him, but he didn't want to parent me.

When parenting became inconvenient, my father chose to leave. And so, he left.

As I grew older, my mom would randomly reveal small details about my father, short anecdotes describing his character. The more I learned about him, the less I desired to know him further.

Eventually, I chose to leave him.

By the time of my father's death, I chose to completely stop speaking to him. For years, he called me, phoning the house he once shared with me and my mother in the suburbs of Philadelphia. I am told that my father was charming, and that when engaged or truly excited about something, his blue eyes crinkled and shined the same way mine would years later.

It was at eleven years old that I decided I no longer needed to answer the sporadic calls my father made to our home's landline phone. The job he initially left me for in Indiana later transitioned into a move to Florida (to be closer to his parents, ha!).

He now seemed to have no intention of coming home whatsoever.

Even now, I don't understand his irresponsibility and lack of interest in being a parent. I don't understand how my own mother, the most responsible and at times controlling person I know, could even fall in love with someone like my father. It's weird to admit that I don't really know my father. As a child, I didn't give him the opportunity to get to know me either.

The stories I heard of other women, of drinking, and the utmost rejection I felt at his going away was what ultimately led to my own silence. It feels empowering to say now that I, a child, had left him, an adult. I know it may not have really been the case but telling myself that makes me feel better.

It's important for me to emphasize that I stopped answering my father's calls not out of pressure from my mother or out of service to anybody other than myself.

At a certain point, whenever I walked through our kitchen, I would just look at our landline phone with a strange veneer of disgust, as if it were a cockroach that somehow snuck its way into our house. That landline phone was symbolic of a life where my father was consistently out of reach. His was a presence that I yearned for, but also turned myself against.

Eventually, we got rid of that phone.

So that August afternoon, when I learned of my father's death, I held my knees close to my chest and backed into our dining room wall, suddenly afraid of the real world, the real world where I now had truly lost one parent forever.

Suddenly, the world felt surreal. Even now, I think his death hurts more than the loss of the man himself. All I knew was that our relationship could never be fixed. The damage was irreparable. I knew that no bridge between the two of us could ever be rebuilt.

The permanency of his loss grounded me in a way that I had never experienced before, now at the age of fourteen. The sporadic phone calls I ignored then now seemed to collect all around me, enveloping me in this strange, weighted blanket of guilt and grief. Everything had finally collapsed at my feet.

~

Just four months later, the crisp smell of evergreen trees hung loosely in the air. My mom and I had just returned from Tanners, a local, farm-owned grocery store, with this year's Christmas tree strapped tightly to the trunk of our car. I named the tree "Garfunkel," in a quirky homage to what I believed was the often less-revered half of Simon & Garfunkel.

It was December fifth, a little less than four months after my father's death, and things were already abuzz in preparation for the upcoming holidays.

Now fifteen years old, it was my job to haul our Christmas tree into the house. I hoisted and turned it in the air while my mom searched for "the good side," and I could finally set the tree down firmly into its stand. A flood of dense green needles quickly spread across our living room floor, making their way into the crevices between the crown moulding and carpeting, later to be found deep beneath our matching red sofas.

At this rate, the winter sun had disappeared on the two of us hours ago, and the entire first floor of our townhouse was enveloped by the yellow glow cast by our dining room's overhead light fixture. Outside, out past our living room blinds, the world had become an eerie and wintry pitch-black blue. But before we could even begin to vacuum, or God forbid string any twinkling lights or ornaments along our Christmas tree, my mother whispered to me quietly:

"I need to tell you something."

Though firm in tone, and ultimately in line with her characteristic directness, it was unusual for my mother to say something so softly.

Barely detectable in her voice was the same pain I heard in the "I need to tell you something" she greeted me with on the afternoon of my father's death. Again, I felt the blood quickly rush to my ears, as my eyes lazily adjusted to my surroundings.

Together, the two of us sat at our dining room table, again, side by side. A foreboding sense of déjà vu seeped within my bones, and I couldn't help but feel nervous as I sat there next to her.

"Something to tell me. What could it be?" I thought.

"The other week I was diagnosed with colon cancer. I am going to be okay, it is not that serious, and I am going to get surgery to remove it in a few weeks. It is going to be okay." Though her voice remained calm, her eyes darted about nervously.

"Oh," was all I could muster in reply.

Immediately, I centered the situation around myself.

Would I become an orphan? What did this mean?

How sick was my mom? Who would take care of me if she died?

Both parents, in the same year? Really?

Oh my God, she looks so scared. I can see it in her eyes. Oh my God. Oh my God. Ok, try to put on a brave face.

Try Liz, c'mon.

CHAPTER 2

A SONG IN TWO PARTS

DAD

I am six years old sitting in the passenger seat of my dad's red pickup truck, listening to the gravel crunch as he barrels us toward his cabin in the woods. We are somewhere in rural Pennsylvania. Somewhere I don't know the name of even now. The dark is coming, and the trees feel as though they're caving in on us. I'm not scared, sitting there loosely strapped into the passenger seat. I'm a big girl. I hear the gravel crunch beneath his car tires, and I forever associate that sound with nervous excitement. This sound means it's a weekend with my dad.

We pull up to the cabin and I half trip my way out of the truck, bouncing with glee. Here I can eat Pringles and Cocoa Puffs and play video games featuring SpongeBob. Here we can eat and say and do anything mom HATES. Here we watch the movie *Men in Black*, although I am not the biggest fan. We also watch old John Wayne movies that I really don't care for and my dad will drink beer and I will become quiet because now, after the beer, he is quiet himself.

My dad will drink several beers and fall asleep on the couch while my small little body curls up on the couch adjacent to his. I silently urge him to wake up and go back to the one bedroom this small cabin has, quietly hoping he will get up so I can be alone.

I only want to be alone sometimes. On other days, I hope my father stays asleep on the couch adjacent to mine and never leaves.

If only that were the case.

When it is finally time to sleep, I am frustrated because the couches are ratty and old. There is no support or backing to the couch arms, so you can't lay your head on the couch even if you wanted to sleep. Following my father's lead, I would wedge a pillow into a corner of the couch as he had taught me. Yet almost every night, it would slip through the giant crack and my head would lightly bang the wood railing beneath it.

I would wake up throughout the night as my head would literally knock on wood. It was the gentle sting of childhood frustration.

"Please dad," I whispered desperately. I knew that if I complained enough, my dad would let me have the big queen-sized bed in the cabin's single bedroom all to myself. But mostly, I tried not to complain. This was dad's weekend after all.

~

My father and I would often spend our weekends together fishing on these little row boats or fishing on the dock, sometimes venturing into a sort of community center for fishermen afterwards. On our trips, I was always allowed to pick a snack from the vending machine. It was my special prize for putting up with my father's hobby and for complaining only a little bit. I remember always being on my best behavior throughout my time with my father because I knew how limited that time could be.

My mother did not get this benefit.

Without a doubt, when given the option, I would *always* choose Cheetos for my afternoon fishing snack. Cheetos and the orange cheddar-y dust on my fingertips served as a scrumptious source of pride.

On one of those afternoons out on the lake with my father, I surprised the both of us by catching a fish. It was a tiny little fish, but I was so proud of myself because I had caught a fish and my father hadn't. I was prideful, even then. Time and time again, my father boasted of his excellent fisherman skills and how much of a man he was and now, his six-year-old daughter, his only child, was the only one of us to succeed.

I was thrilled, even as the first wintry frosts of resentment toward my father began to work their way into my veins.

"We have to put it back," my father said gruffly.

Put it back? But this was my big catch!

"Why?" I asked, hurt seeping into my voice.

"Because it's too small, Elizabeth. We need to," he replied.

The fact was, every catch my father had ever made was savored and relished, every fish his "best catch yet."

Disappointed and bitter, I dragged my feet the entire way back home.

I trudged out here to this lake with my father every other weekend for as long as I could remember. I had trudged myself out to this lake every other weekend just hoping to catch a fish and make my father proud—and once I finally did, he hardly seemed to notice.

There were, of course, good memories too.

Around Christmas of that same year, I spent part of the holidays with my father and his sister's family, feeling as festive and happy as my six-year-old self could possibly feel. When it was time to bake some Christmas cookies, instead of making the traditional chocolate chip, my dad suggested we try making snickerdoodles.

"Snickerdoodles?" I said with an incredulous, little kid laugh. The word sounded so preposterous and silly that I couldn't help but laugh.

"Snickerdoodles, snickerdoodles, snickerdoodles!" I yelled with glee.

"Snickerdoodles!" my dad laughed back. "Here, let me show you."

For as long as I knew him, my father loved showing me how to do things with my hands. My mom does this too, but this is the form of love I remember receiving most from my dad while he was alive.

Let me teach you how to fish. Let me show you how to make snickerdoodles. My pride might be conditional depending on my mood, but nevertheless, I will teach you. Here is all you can do in the world through the work of your hands.

While in the end, my father didn't have much to offer me, what he did give to me, I have never forgotten.

Making snickerdoodles was fun and lighthearted; the magic of cinnamon sugar dust and warm crisp cookies formed a bond of love and baking and home that would settle within me for a lifetime. I remember the smell, the yellow glow cast over my aunt's kitchen as the winter sun dipped down low and brought in the night.

These few pages are the most that I have openly talked about my father in many years. I have so few memories of my dad, and even fewer not frosted with resentment, that telling anybody in my life something positive about him felt like I was giving those few good memories away.

By sharing him with other people, I was betraying that younger and more naïve part of myself, or maybe more simply, it felt like a betrayal to my mom and the hard work of raising me on her own. Snickerdoodles were my precious memory, but to most just a common cookie. I would bake for my friends whenever I was feeling sentimental and often requested them from the (not so good) cookie shop I frequented throughout my four years in college.

Before my dad died, all I ever thought of were memories like that afternoon fishing out on the lake and of the sporadic birthday cards I later received in the mail as a teenager. Memories laced with weight and disappointment clouded my thoughts of him—and without new ones to replace them with, I didn't know where else to turn.

I thought of all the gifts my dad sent to me in an attempt to buy my love, and of the landline calls I eventually stopped answering. I was not as actively angry or pissed off with my father by the time he died because I simply didn't know him any longer.

I didn't know my own father and as uncomfortable as a truth that was to confront, it was the only one I had at my disposal. There was simply no other option.

Now that he's dead, I still think of afternoons fishing and of my head slipping through the sofa cracks in his cabin. I think of struggling to fall asleep at night, lying a few feet away from him in the dark. But I also still wonder about our snickerdoodle cookies and our matching blue eyes and giggling over sour cream and onion Pringles or Cocoa Puffs cereal with a pirated copy of *The Incredibles* movie.

Now I see his selfishness and his immaturity, his struggles with alcoholism while still portraying a boyish charm and stringent pride. I see the tenderness, the almost childish innocence, and his desire to be strong even though he wasn't. I see a man with all his flaws, and I see the remnants of a child.

In my father, I see myself, and everything I have ever wanted, and everything I don't want to be.

I hope one day to drive down to Florida and find my father's grave. I hope to find him wherever he may be these days. To simply say hello. He never went searching for me for the last seven years of his life, and I kept the door to my heart locked tight with a key.

On some days, I wish I had left the door cracked open a bit. I know on most days, that it's better I did not.

MOM

Dear Elizabeth, 10/13/15

I love you so much. It's hard to describe in words the love I have for you. It is something so special and wonderful you just know it has to be a gift from God. No one else could have created something so beautiful and miraculous as you. I am truly blessed to be your Mom. You are a miracle! And I am not using that word loosely at all. Do you know how I always told you how you are named after your great grandmom Elizabeth because she gave me you? I feel now is a good time to explain that a little more than I already have. It is such a beautiful story....

We tried for a long time to have you and things just weren't working out. For many reasons, we were about to give up trying to have a baby and I was praying a lot during that time. Your great grandmom Elizabeth was in a nursing home at this time, 92 years old, alert and fairly healthy. I visited her on a fairly regular basis but one day I had an overwhelming feeling that I just had to see her. It kept nagging at me all day so much so that I convinced your dad to delay leaving for a trip that evening so he could visit too. We had a great visit and your dad left for his trip. As I was saying goodbye to her, she said goodnight and then she suddenly got this great big smile on her face – something that was unusual. It was the kind of smile that looked like it held a secret. That she knew something that I didn't know. I went home that night and was thinking about that smile and the phone rang and I was informed that she had passed away in her sleep. Not too soon after I discovered I was pregnant! I couldn't believe it! Exactly the day she died you were conceived! A miracle! She had left this earth to give me you and that smile was her knowing what God had planned! This event was the beginning of what will always be the best part of my life: Having you as my child, raising you has been the best experience of my life. Each day I am reminded of what a wonderful, loving, smart and compassionate girl you are and I thank God a thousand times for giving me you!

As you know, these past few years have been very difficult for us. We lost grandmom 3 years ago, our 15 yr old dog Sierra Louise died 2 years ago and your Dad died last year. A few months after his death, I get informed that I have cancer. At that time, I am really angry with God. I don't get it. I am not praying to him anymore. I am praying to our Blessed Mother. Maybe she can fix all this. After all she is a Mom, she will understand...I go into "auto pilot" mode. I put one foot in front of the other and just keep going. You and I talk about it sometimes but at first I am just trying to get thru each day. It is all about me now. I am getting a lot of medical tests, I am trying to work as much as I can amid surgeries and treatments. I am trying to keep your world as normal as I can. It is very hard to do that as a single parent with very little family help. I am dependent on you now for certain things and I feel really bad about that. During this time you encourage me to go to Sunday mass when I am able. I am so grateful that you do! I need the encouragement. I need to pray. But I don't notice that you are struggling too. Not only about me being sick but also with your Dad's death. What I notice is this great kid who has grown up so much this past year, who kept her studies going amongst all this chaos, and who, despite all this disruption, continued to make me so proud of her! You did it all with no complaints. I am so thankful. I am amazed at your strength. I am so blessed to have you.

We are slowly starting to get back to normal. You showed (and continue to show) so much strength and maturity. You and I can talk about anything together. As you know, nothing is off-limits. Absolutely nothing. I am so glad that you feel comfortable to talk with me about things. I am so glad that you are receptive to other people you can talk to besides me. That is so good! It is great to get "outside" advice sometimes that include friends, family and professionals. I am thrilled you get to experience Kairos this year. It couldn't have come at a more perfect time! You will be a great leader Elizabeth at Kairos and in anything that you do!

But please, let's not forget God! I know I mentioned earlier how angry I was with God. I didn't want to talk or pray to him anymore. But God spoke to me thru you when you encouraged me to go to Sunday mass when I was getting better. I know in my heart that God is really the only one that can get us thru the tough times. He is always there for us. Even when we don't want him to be. Even when we start to not believe he is there for us. He really is. You helped to show me that Elizabeth. Pray. God hears you.

I knew from the very beginning how special you are Elizabeth and soon you will complete high school and start college. Whatever you choose to study and wherever you go, I know that you will do your best and you will find your way. You are strong. You are opinionated. You are a great writer. You know how proud I am of the article you wrote about us in the Bucks County Courier newspaper. I still cry when I read it and I read it a thousand times! My co-workers cried when they read it and demanded copies! You are passionate about certain things. You are beautiful! (Yes, you are!). You are compassionate. You are tolerant. You are a great hugger and cuddler. You are loveable and you make great scrambled eggs! You are faithful. Your faith will take your far Elizabeth. Beyond your wildest dreams if you let it. I love you "pumpkin"! You're the best!

Love you forever and always,
Mom

~

During my junior year of high school, I was invited to join a religious retreat my school typically restricted to seniors. Juniors with "leadership potential" and "adverse experiences" typically made the cut.

On the second night of our four-day retreat, some of the teachers from our school read surprise letters written to us from our parents. Most of the letters followed the standard: "I love you, I'm so proud of you," guidelines. All of the letters read aloud that night were beautiful.

Yet my letter was different. My letter told our story.

My mom had no idea it would be read aloud, not only to me, but to many of my classmates.

She later felt a little embarrassed about that. I told her not to worry about it.

"I liked sharing our story," I said. "It's a pretty good one."

Listening to the letter read aloud, after listening to so many of the others that came before it, I laid there, surrounded by my classmates, and cried.

If picturing this feels weird, remember this is a religious retreat we're talking about here.

Even so, lying there on the floor in a softly lit room in the middle of a random retreat center in Delaware, I felt whole for the first time in a year as I listened to my mother's version of our story. Hearing her voice, the pain and love and pride mixed in her retelling of our lives, I felt the greatest emotional release I had ever felt.

I looked up at the popcorn ceiling above me and scrunched up my eyes in an attempt to hold onto this moment forever.

CHAPTER 3

DEER

———

A deer stood in front of me, maybe ten feet away, staring at me the way that a dog would. I stuck my tongue out playfully and made my eyes bulge, contorting my face in the same way you want to make a baby laugh. In that moment, the quick thought of company, though feigned, comforted me.

I haven't done this in a long time: writing in the Notes app as I walk around my neighborhood. It's the deer that always spark that little itch in the pit of my stomach, that make the words pour out of my mouth faster than I can type them.

~

For the first few months my mother went through chemo, I immersed myself within the dramatic world of *Grey's Anatomy*. The character of Izzy was quickly my favorite—blonde, blunt, and beautiful.

As her character lay wrapped up in a bubblegum pink dress, arms wrapped around her dying lover, I remember thinking to myself: *This is probably how I should feel about my mom right now.*

Pat, another girl in my writing program, says that I could try writing about how I coped with my dad's death and mother's cancer. For a while, I didn't cope. I watched *Grey's Anatomy*, struggled in my Honors Chemistry class, and fought to put on a brave face in front of my mom and in front of my classmates.

And then the swallowing started. The feeling in my throat. The feeling that all the breath had been taken out of me—paralyzing me with fear.

After my mom was diagnosed, my anxiety reached a new, unparalleled height. My anxiety, if previously dormant, was now frighteningly alive, often physically manifesting in a way that made me feel as if I were choking. The golden crucifix my great grandmother previously wore now felt strained across my collarbone and the contours of my neck. Each night I would lay in bed anticipating the sound of my own ragged breathing. My own fears of death seemed to manifest deep within my throat.

For a while I couldn't be near necklaces and feared the presence of knives, particularly the giant chef's knife in our tiny tidy kitchen, with a small, yet distinct fear that I might hurt myself. Yet after a while, my fears subsided. I learned to trust myself again, and in doing so, toss my greatest fears aside. I was only able to do after I started seeing Dr. F.

I met Dr. F the summer after my sophomore year in high school. She was Italian, so I immediately trusted her, given my background. Dr. F had dark ribbon curls of hair and the intrigued, detached demeanor I assumed a therapist might have. When Dr. F smiled, she smiled wide—but she didn't smile all too frequently. Stern, yet unassuming, Dr. F reminded me of my mother.

It had been my idea to seek out a therapist, after watching one particular episode of *The West Wing*, the popular political drama series.

There's an episode in the second season of the series titled, "Noel." In it, one of the show's central protagonists, Josh, suffers from post-traumatic stress disorder after being shot a few months prior.

As viewers, you watch this charmingly rogue and nearing middle-aged man slowly lose his cool, his center, due to an undiagnosed and ongoing battle with mental illness. Eventually, his coworkers coerce him into seeing a therapist, and after some trepidation, the sessions seem to help. Watching that episode, I knew that some sort of battle was going on inside of me too.

I also wanted to be helped.

In the years since those initial meetings with Dr. F, I have been careful to note and try to lend a hand, when I can see myself or others on the fringes of disassociation or darkness. My efforts to help myself ended up being successful. My efforts to help those around me have not always been met with open arms.

I told Dr. F about the tightness in my chest and my fear of knives and razors and the intrusive thoughts that continued to pop into my head. I finally thought I understood why people hurt themselves, or at least why I imagined I might.

I hadn't.

I wouldn't.

But I liked the idea of controlling what might happen to me—controlling the amount of pain I might be able to feel.

Dr. F gave me breathing exercises and told me to consider regular exercise as a means towards lessening my anxiety. I have always been a talker, and I have always overshared; explaining how I felt to Dr. F never felt particularly difficult for me, just maybe a little bit shameful. My mother raised me to be tough, and the ease in which I could admit my weaknesses at times made me feel small.

I talked to Dr. F for months and months and started losing weight exercising as my mother finished her final rounds of chemotherapy.

In one picture from that summer, I'm standing in front of the famous Pat's and Gino's cheesesteak restaurants in Philadelphia, grinning this wide grin. My legs are wrinkly with fat as my tie dye t-shirt clings to the breasts that will disappear with time. My mother, my Aunt Shell, her best friend, and I had just gone to Jefferson University Hospital for a second opinion. My mother's doctors at Fox Chase Cancer Center suggested she start radiation after she finished chemotherapy. My mother refused to consider it. To her, enough was enough. The chemo would work as best as it could, and that would be the end of that.

~

As I write this, it's now six years later and I'm back watching the deer in my neighborhood, writing as many of my thoughts down as I can. As the group of eight (or was it nine?) deer graze in the grass before me, one watches me type and wags his tail. I'm glad I don't scare them.

I wonder how Dr. F's doing. I hope she's doing well.

Taking a deep breath by myself, surrounded by stillness, I realize in this moment how glad I am to be home. How glad I am that like this family of animals—my mom and I remain together, forever our two-person home.

CHAPTER 4

ENGLISH

———

"Liz, will your mom and dad be joining us?" asked my Honors English teacher one morning.

We had been back to school for a few weeks now, and I had slowly begun to tell my friends about my father's recent passing. Back-to-school night was an annual tradition for the parents of my school—a night where they could come in to visit our teachers, learn more about our syllabi and discover what we'd all be learning throughout that year.

I was determined not to show weakness in front of my friends, but especially amongst my more competitive friends in my Honors English and Honors U.S. History classes.

"No, Mr. Turner, my father is dead," I replied to him curtly.

A hush fell over our small classroom.

I spent my four years of high school at a private, Catholic, all-girls academy in Northeast Philadelphia. Formerly a convent, the building loomed like a fortress from the outside. Grey stone bricks built up four stories that led to the bell tower we were forbidden to climb. Increasingly insecure with my friendships, I wondered how anyone would take me seriously if let my guard down. I chose to conflate my own pain with weakness, but I wasn't sure why. Would my friends still like me if I didn't come from a family that looked like theirs?

Going to Catholic school and growing up with a single mom, I sometimes felt that my classmates looked at me as though I were damaged goods. If I was the "before," picture, then they were the "after."

Throughout those first few weeks of my sophomore year, I felt myself internally breaking down —slowly developing a tendency towards constant weariness, ready to snap at the smallest inconvenience or perceived indiscretion. Over time, I would slowly disassociate from my surroundings and fellow classmates entirely.

~

Even now, I don't fully understand how my father died. My paternal grandparents told us it was due to complications from non-Hodgkin's lymphoma, the same form of cancer my father had in his thirties.

My mother speculated that his death was partially due to a cancer recurrence—that his alcoholic tendencies and unhealthy eating habits probably had their own role to play. I've never seen my father's death certificate, so I've never had a real or concrete answer.

What I do know is that now, in what feels like eons later, when I asked my mother why we had never gone to my father's funeral, she simply told me: "We weren't invited."

~

Back in the classroom, I felt little to no remorse in vocalizing my father's death out loud, or in feeling the blank and shocked stares of my classmates as their eyes bore into me.

I felt nothing towards my poor teacher scrambling to come up with a sympathetic response.

I was numb to it all, or at least I tried to convince myself that I was.

The truth is, I was all too aware of my surroundings—and relished in the attention my outburst gave me. If anything, I was honestly a bit amused with myself.

The year before, I had worked to establish myself as the bold, often dynamic class clown within our tight-knit Honors English circle.

Maybe now I had some depth. I cared so much about what that specific group of teenage girls thought of me. They were my competition, my friends, and to some degree, my closest family.

Intergroup dynamics had quickly proved themselves to be important throughout my high school experience, and projecting confidence to the other girls around me was key. I believed that by acting confidently and cracking sardonic jokes about my father's death, I could assert myself as a figure of character amongst my friends. I was never going to be in the honors or AP science and math classes—that was one thing I knew for sure. Maybe my newly developed morose sense of humor could set me apart. In this way, I would be special.

There were more incidences during my sophomore year beyond that day in English class. The more that winter bore on, the colder and crasser I became.

At the time, I didn't care who I upset or frustrated with my lack of empathy, and often blatant disregard. I was miserable and wanted everyone else to feel my pain. To some degree, I wanted them to be miserable with me.

~

A few months into the school year, my mom revealed to me her initial cancer diagnosis. After just barely confiding in my friends about the loss of my father, I now started to share my mother's diagnosis.

In truth, I didn't know how to navigate those initial conversations, much less know how to keep my friends updated on our situation as it inevitably progressed.

One afternoon, I decided to share my news with a few of my friends during our lunch period.

One of these friends was a girl named Jade.

Jade was blonde, somewhat shy, and doe like in every respect—the image of mousy innocence to every adult that met her, but an intellectual powerhouse to the classmates that often competed with her, including myself.

I wasn't sure how I felt about Jade. Something about her rubbed me the wrong way throughout my time in high school, though for the most part, she was always friendly to me. Throughout that sophomore spring, Jade seemed to think my gruff honesty was cool, or something to be quietly respected, which I appreciated.

At the same time, our one-on-one conversations always felt stagnant—the both of us seeming to take turns congratulating the other on whatever recent achievement they'd had in a show of faux modesty.

As I shared my mother's diagnosis, Jade immediately said to me, "Well, my dad had colon cancer a few years ago and he's just fine now."

A triumphant little smile. *"See Liz, I beat ya to it."*

I think, in some immature and perverse type of way, she was attempting to comfort me.

A sort of *"You can get through this, too! I'm sure you can!"* with a flash of Jade's signature pearly white teeth.

It felt as though she had completely dismissed my experience. A *"You're not special."*

If I hadn't felt so lonely at the time, I'm not sure I would have cared so much.

My heart sank and a short-fused anger started to rise in my stomach like bile, threatening to break loose.

There was nothing snarky I could say in response to Jade without likely being ratted on to a beloved teacher or God forbid, one of the nuns that ran our school. All I could think of in the moment was the fact that Jade had another parent, and three younger siblings to help out or lean on for some form of comfort.

Our experiences were not the same.

I was, and am, all my mother had.

Choosing to keep my mouth closed for once, I opted for a sullen look of disgust and went back to my lunch, ignoring Jade for the rest of the day, and possibly the rest of the week.

That outburst in English class and lunchtime conversation with Jade were typical throughout my sophomore year of high school.

For a while afterwards, I refused to forgive the classmates that watched me struggle and writhe that year. The solitude I felt, the weight of living in that experience so seemingly alone, led to the slow decay of more than a few friendships over time.

It wasn't their job to understand. It wasn't my job to make them.

I know this now, but I didn't know that then.

"Liz, will your mom and dad be joining us?" asked Mr. Turner.

"My mom will," I wish I had said. "And that's more than enough."

CHAPTER 5

YELLOW SOCKS

———

Throughout that winter, I slowly started telling my friends about my mom's cancer in hushed whispers across the lunchroom—these friends being the same girls I had often been abrasive and defensive with throughout the last few months.

"My mom is sick," is just about all I could let out. I could give no serious explanation, nor could I reveal any details. I honestly hadn't been given any about her diagnosis other than "It's not too bad," and I desperately didn't want to confront the news too seriously myself.

But by my third day back at school that very first week, my body was so wrought with anxiety and stress that I had made myself physically sick. I threw up in the middle of health class in front of all of my classmates, feeling absolutely weak and mortified by what had just happened.

I had barely told anyone what was going on in my life just yet, and those that I had told had nothing to say.

We were fifteen, I think to myself now. *How could they even begin to know what to say?*

After a trip to the nurse's office, I was promptly sent home and picked up by my overly concerned mom.

"This is due to the stress, isn't it?" She asked me, as sorrow filled her eyes.

I didn't deny it.

"It'll all be okay," I said instead back to her, with a sheepish smile. "I'm sorry you had to take off of work."

"No, that's okay. Now we can both play hooky."

My own treatment at home, the throwing up had signified and later escalated into a fever, involved chicken noodle soup and Ritz crackers and blue Gatorade.

Nestled into a temporary cocoon in our living room for the rest of the school week, I had no idea how my mom's strenuous chemotherapy regimen would come to affect our lives just a few months later.

The surgery to remove my mom's tumor would happen less than ten days before Christmas.

Her favorite sister, my Aunt Jamie, took a train up from Virginia Beach to stay with me while my mom recovered in the hospital. My Aunt Shell, my mom's best friend from the age of sixteen onward, went with the two of them to the hospital while I spent the day at school.

"I want everything to be as normal for you as possible," my mother insisted on the day of her surgery and in the weeks and months that followed.

"I want your life to be as normal as possible."

But already I knew that it wouldn't be.

Her diagnosis was something unalterable that had not only happened to her, but had happened to our family, and had completely changed the day-to-day structure of our lives.

The thing about having any procedures done related to the colon is that the body has to be completely cleared out of all foods and liquids—not including water. This meant that in the days leading up to her colon cancer surgery, my mom couldn't eat or drink anything, except for this milky solution prescribed to her by her doctors.

I watched as she became gradually weaker and weaker days before she ever checked into the hospital.

If my writing seems unemotional, or maybe even clinical and impersonal in its descriptions, it is because I truly haven't addressed or thought about these details in years.

From that instant, I was already working on blocking all of this out and pushing it to the very hidden most corners of my mind.

Throughout the next few months, I would slowly start to completely disassociate from what I knew to be my life, and it is that winter, that all these years later, I still hardly remember at all.

This is when the yellow hospital socks first came into my life.

Upon any patient's eventual release from the hospital, hospital staff will typically allow the patient to take home a nice pair of non-skid, cozy hospital socks in addition to the ones that they used throughout their stay.

I used to think that maybe this was a sweet deal that my mom had gotten for having her surgery at a decently revered cancer specialty hospital. I used to think that maybe her nurses had favored her above some of their rowdier, more demanding patients.

With time, I realized that the socks were just a courtesy provided to everyone, another protocol mandated by the hospital, designed to increase patient satisfaction. Whatever the case may be, the two or three pairs of yellow hospital socks my mom was sent home with that December changed her life temporarily and changed mine forever.

That year, I learned my first real lesson on being an adult: your life is no longer simply about you. In a million small ways, you can devote yourself to bettering the lives of others. Be selfless. Try.

I write "the first lesson" but I don't have a set or written down series of lessons on being an adult. I'm only twenty-one years old, and honestly very much in the beginnings of figuring this all out for myself.

Still, this learned idea of selflessness was a learned maturity and welcome into adulthood that I could have only gained through something as traumatic and emotionally draining as my mom's colon cancer diagnosis.

At fifteen, I learned, out of necessity, the very beginnings of being an adult and how to be a real human of character, something other than an angsty only child who only does whatever they want whenever they want to do it.

My adolescent turn towards selflessness revolved around those yellow hospital socks, and I don't think the lesson could've truly taken root without them.

A typical day that winter of 2015 would go like this: I would wake myself up at 5:30 a.m., walk over to catch my first bus to school by 5:50 p.m., later transfer to a second bus around 6:30 a.m., and finally get to school around 7:15 a.m.

I would sit complacently throughout my classes all day, expounding the only energy I had in either cracking what I believed to be righteously sardonic jokes or developing a grievous insecurity within most of my friendships.

Then I would go on to sing in three separate choir groups after school, two days a week.

On those days, I'd then take the "late bus" home from school and not get home until 5:30 p.m. (if I was lucky), and not until 6 p.m. on the very worst days. The rush hour Philadelphia traffic could really get hairy, depending on the day.

At times, sitting in our dining room by myself, I would solemnly guzzle down a quick dinner, likely leftovers or some sort of takeout, and continue to check on my mom throughout the rest of the night in between studying and homework and way too many checks of my burgeoning social media feeds.

I would then spend whatever remaining free time I had watching *Grey's Anatomy* or *Gilmore Girls.*

Grey's Anatomy in particular I still strongly associate with my mother's cancer. On weeknights, weekends and with every free moment I had, I watched the show with my heart on my sleeve, feeling the pain of a character's death or sickness more deeply than I possibly could with that of my father or mother.

I was entrenched within the complex, almost-generational character arcs, and deeply entranced — at one point watching ten seasons of the medical drama in roughly twenty-eight days.

That same spring following my mom's initial surgery, she needed my help with almost everything.

Her body was in serious recovery, healing from the hours-long procedure that had removed her tumor and a larger portion of her colon itself.

She was physically weaker than she had ever been before, and the prospect of chemotherapy still awaited us.

So, every night, my mom would look at me with pleading eyes and ask me to help her put on her yellow hospital socks so that her feet could stay warm as she went to sleep.

I'm ashamed to admit that in the early days of our new schedule, I complained frequently about having to help my mom with the smallest of things.

I had already entered the part of teenagerdom that desperately yearned for an increased independence—which of course now seemed impossible. At times I was likely a little bit resentful. Where was my childhood? My teenage years?

My sophomore year of high school?

Would things ever go back to normal?

I felt as though the remainder of my teenage years had suddenly vanished in a flash, and it was only fate or an unfavorable God I could find to blame.

Throughout my short life, I had been found to be actively, maybe even naturally selfish, but the small act of service I chose to do each night for my mother was not.

So, every night, I slipped a well-worn pair of yellow hospital socks onto my mother's cold and tired feet, and I kissed her goodnight. I pushed aside my own bitterness and feelings and finally put someone else—not to mention the person who loved me most in the world—ahead of myself, even if only for a few short moments.

And even on our hardest of days, it always felt good. I always felt better after putting those yellow socks on my mother's feet and tucking her into bed.

Now that it had come down to it, I could be the mom.

I could take care of her now.

So, that next phase of my life started to begin, accompanied by a few pairs of yellow hospital socks and an article in the local newspaper highlighting this new ritual my mother and I had formed together.

I wrote about my hope to turn towards selflessness and how "the c word," had impacted our small family. My article was for whoever had the interest in reading my words and in learning our story. But mostly, I still wrote selfishly.

I wrote mostly for myself.

A smiling picture of my mom and I from the summer before accompanied the newspaper article, and while she was still able to go to work, my mom passed the article around to all of her co-workers.

"My baby wrote this," she would say to anybody who dared to stop by her cubicle. "You should read it."

I was and never will be referred to as Liz by my mother, and as Elizabeth only on formal occasions.

I have always been "baby," "pumpkin," "snootch," and a million other names for all of my life.

I expect that I always will be.

My mother, on the other hand? My mother has always been my joy.

CHAPTER 6

ICE

———

"Please, Elizabeth, I need you to come into the bathroom," I heard my mother whisper. "I think I have an infection from the surgery."

It was a few weeks after my mother's tumor was removed. So far, her recovery had been smooth sailing. Tonight, would prove to be a crucial turning point.

Like a siren, a sudden wailing began—bouncing off the walls of our small townhouse.

I admit that I wanted to ignore it at first. Not out of a callousness towards my mother, but because in dealing with her pain, I knew I often couldn't give her the support she deserved. I felt as though my support wasn't enough, and sometimes angry that I had been put in this position as her primary caretaker and comforter.

I was fifteen years old, and all I wanted to do was figure out how to save her. I never knew quite what to do.

Instead, I often tensed up—frozen in place, unable, though not unwilling to come to her rescue.

By now I had become accustomed to the yelps I often heard from my mother's bedroom. I had developed a sort of internal barometer of their severity.

Were her yells loud enough to wake me up?

How long had she been keeping at it?

Was she calling for me now, or trying to stifle the sound of her own voice?

I knew instantly how desperately she needed me that night.

I ran into the bathroom to find her hysterical with pain and grief.

"You're going to be alright," I said, my voice cracking. "Just breathe with me now. You're going to be alright."

"It hurts," she told me.

"What hurts?" I asked.

"Everything hurts," she admitted in defeat, sweat plastering her hair against her forehead, her face flushed red.

We sat there together as I urged her to take deep breaths.

In. Out.

In. Out.

The bathroom's harsh fluorescent lighting made it feel as though we were back in the hospital again. Looking at my mother now, her face bright red with tears streaming down her face, I knew we would be headed back there soon.

It was only a matter of time. How long could I keep her calm and stay with her? How long would it be until someone else could come to our aid?

As helplessness began to set in, I urged myself not to cry.

Crying will only make things worse, I reminded myself.

Crying will only make things worse.

After a short while of sitting in the bathroom together, my mom found the strength to walk the short distance back to her bedroom, though her pain had hardly subsided.

"We still need to call an ambulance," she said. "I think this is from the surgery and we need to figure out what it is."

Close to an hour later, an ambulance finally pulled up to our front lawn. It was an icy night out, wintry, even, the remnants of a storm now several days in the past determined to continue leaving its mark. I shivered, still in my school sweater and jumper, as my mother urged me to pack my backpack for the night and get my things ready for tomorrow's school day.

"I want to come with you," I pleaded. The thought of leaving her alone in the middle of the night to some unforeseen fate felt impossible, if not unavoidable, knowing my mother.

"No, you have school in the morning. You'll stay with a neighbor. I love you. I'll be okay, Elizabeth."

Though it pained me to agree to this plan, I knew that doing so would only relieve my mother. She didn't want me to see her in any more pain.

In our panic, we turned to the first friendly (or at least semi-friendly) faces we could think of: our neighbors.

My mom told me I'd be able to stay with the family of a young girl I used to play with every Saturday afternoon. I remember feeling awkward, knowing that as we'd grown older, we were no longer friends.

That night, as my mother's ambulance flew across I-95, the streets of Philadelphia, and towards her cancer center, our neighbors set up a few sheets and blankets for me on their couch. It took me ten minutes to walk the short distance from my house to theirs, due to the icy sidewalks that threatened the limited traction beneath my scuffed school shoes.

I had never changed out of my uniform, though it was now past 10 p.m.

Years later, my mother would tell me: "The ambulance drivers were barreling down Roosevelt Boulevard blasting

Christmas music. I remember that so strongly, as if it were yesterday."

"The hospital charged me for all of these check-ups they claimed they did during that ambulance ride, but I just remember bracing myself and trying not to yell out in pain as we flew over potholes," she continued.

"The ambulance drivers seemed to think we were all just having fun."

I felt myself tense up at her description of that night. A protective anger welled up inside of me.

I should've gone with her, I thought to myself.

I should have just gone with her.

Once I'd arrived at my neighbor's home that night, they quickly made my presence feel like an inconvenience. The mother of the family gave a few sparing words of consolation before turning upstairs to her own bed, but I could feel discomfort radiating off her in waves.

"I'm sure your mom will be okay, Elizabeth. Try not to worry," she told me. Though her eyes were warm, her smile was small and tentative—as if in this one moment, her character itself was written across her face.

I nodded back at her to signify my understanding, and silently waited for her to go back upstairs for the night.

As soon as she left, I tugged on my pajamas, and cried myself to sleep.

CHAPTER 7

DC STATEHOOD

———

I couldn't fall asleep the night I first met Will.

I was tan and aglow with the thrill of my first day, leading a student organization advocating for DC statehood. Still relaxed and mentally enjoying our final days of warmer weather, I found myself now a sophomore in college, and the first week or so of classes made it feel as though life had finally clicked into place.

I was now living with two of my closest friends in a cramped apartment-style dorm, and one of them had begrudgingly walked over with me to our friend Paul's dorm for yet another Friday night of drinking and laughing and pretending that we were real adults. We had all been friends throughout our freshman year of college and were excited for the newfound excitement and glee that came with being yet another year older.

It was September 7, 2018. My roommate and I came in with the rain.

Walking in, I noticed Will immediately. He was one of Paul's new roommates and one of the few people there that I hadn't known previously.

Blonde, dressed in a plaid flannel, and reading David Hume during the fledgling beginnings of a college dorm party, he immediately looked out of place.

"What the hell are you doing reading right now?" quipped my roommate.

"You know, just catching up on my philosophy," said Will in response.

I felt myself smirk at him from a casual distance. Nevertheless, his eyes quickly found mine.

Before long, we were swapping stories about our families, the summer jobs we'd had, and the types of books we liked to read. Hours passed by in the blink of an eye as our friends sat in an awkward circle in our periphery, drinking rum and coke out of red solo cups.

My girlfriends went as far as to create a group chat from across the room, texting me to relay:

"Will is clearly into you!"

"Clearly" felt like a bit of an overstatement to me. No boy was ever clearly into me, at least in my opinion.

"Oldest of eight?" I asked Will in disbelief during that first conversation.

"I'm an only child."

At one point, in the middle of our conversation and with our small party still fully going on around us, Will got up and pulled a slab of venison out of his freezer to cook. This was a weird thing to do in the middle of a party, much less to cook something like venison in a shabby in-unit dorm kitchen.

Still, I was so instantly smitten with Will, I hardly noticed every eccentricity. For the first time in my life, the air around me suddenly felt electric.

Who was this guy?

When could I see him again?

Was he as interested in me as I was in him?

Why the hell was he cooking venison at ten o'clock on a Friday night?

I remember asking him that final question on that very first night.

"Because I want to—why not?"

Even now, I can still picture the casual shrug of his shoulders that must have followed, and the charming sort of pout he gave to emphasize his chill persona. He was desperately trying to pull off a "Who cares?" type of attitude that I could immediately sense wasn't him.

In fact, Will cared about everything and had some sort of opinion on most things. Even if delving into a discussion on politics, religion, or gender made our relationship tense at times, I always valued how greatly he seemed to care, and wanted others to know that he cared, too.

But on that rainy September night however, he was all Joe Cool.

~

I left Paul and Will's dorm after a few hours of semi-casual conversation before almost anyone else had left, decidedly intent on going to bed early and getting a good night of sleep. This was the kind of college student that I was.

I didn't get Will's phone number before I left and he didn't get mine, but he was my friend's roommate, and I was sure our paths would cross again.

They had to, didn't they?

But instead of getting the rest I'd hoped for, I tossed and turned in bed for hours, thinking of this handsome blonde guy that had the confidence and ease of a budding politician, or handsome young country singer, or maybe even both.

All I knew was that I wanted to know more.

I saw Will the next week for a walk to the Washington Monument, and then a few days later, and soon all my wildest hopes were confirmed.

He liked me just as much as I liked him.

It feels almost juvenile to phrase it this way now, but it was probably the most exciting thing that had ever happened to me at the time.

Will kissed me first, only after a semi-obvious attempt to shoo away his roommates, and later asked me out (after I had first asked, only half-joking: "So are you gonna ask me out or what?").

Very quickly, we were boyfriend and girlfriend. We became the mom and dad of our budding and newly conjoined friend group. We were the old people that read Hume and went to bed early on a Friday night. We were an us.

Will and I were quick to find one another in every free moment that fall—building encyclopedias of each other in our minds, constantly letting out one of those sweet sighs that comes with falling in love, earnest and eager in our every interaction.

I met his parents and oldest sister, the second of his family's eight, when his cousin got married at the Washington National Cathedral that November. I was immediately intimidated and in awe of his family. I was intimidated by their size and their meaning to Will, as well as their socioeconomic status and my perceived sense of their prestige.

I had never so desperately wanted to be liked in my life. I had never been so cognizant of how I had grown up, and of what my family looked like.

Will's parents were considerably younger than my mom, and throughout that first encounter with them, I didn't know how to interact like a normal, functioning human being. Meeting them made the secret smiles that Will and I often exchanged feel more meaningful.

I will never forget the knot of nervousness that formed in my stomach when I instinctively went to grab Will's hand and saw a quick smile flash across his mother's face. My first seal of approval. With time, I would truly fall in love with Will's family too.

Later that wedding weekend, Will asked me to go on a walk—just the two of us —around campus and who knows where else. We had just grabbed dinner together a few hours beforehand.

Deep in my gut, I knew what was about to follow.

I knew that I was in love with him and that he was likely in love with me, too. But how could I know for sure? Who would bite the bullet and just say it already? We were stubborn and smitten and nervous all at once.

I now know that Will's intention was for the two of us to walk down to the White House and for him to tell me he loved me for the very first time right there. This was the grand plan from the king of grand plans.

Only, fortunately, given my thoughts on who had then resided in the White House, the moment didn't exactly come to fruition in that way. We made it as far as the General Services Administration, the federal agency that helps run other federal agencies.

We were a mere few blocks away from the White House, when beneath a small tree, Will turned to me, and simply couldn't keep it in any longer.

There was a beautiful preamble he gave me, with a feeling of surreal elation and *is this really happening?* coursing throughout my body. And then he said it.

"I love you, Liz. I'm in love with you."

Shocked to actually hear what I had felt from him finally spoken aloud, it took me a half second to respond and say it back to him. Life itself felt as though it made the quick change from sepia to technicolor.

The clichés I had read about and seen in movies and heard in love songs all seemed to be true.

We were in love, and I wanted to tell everyone I knew and had yet to meet, from that monster in the White House to anyone in the DC metro area that would listen. *We were in love.*

The next year and a half of our lives saw countless adventures (across both states and continents), countless firsts, fights, promise rings, his family fully becoming my family, tears of all kinds, lots and lots of dates, desserts to always be split in two, and finally,- an untimely ending.

A year and a half later, neither one of us was even nearly the same person the other had first fallen in love with. Will had lost confidence in himself, in me and in the dreams we worked to build together.

I felt the spark diminish and his interest in me lessen, so I fought for our relationship tooth and nail, sometimes at the cost of myself.

In those final months we were together, I made myself feel small in order to keep Will around and his doubts about me at bay. On other days, I lashed out at him and would strike back at whatever perceived injustice, lack of care, or lack of time I felt I had been dealt.

The days of lying around in bed for an entire afternoon, the only two people on Earth—those days had long passed for the two of us. But still, this person had become my home.

Still, I absolutely loved him.

How could I let that go?

When Will came to my dorm room and told me "I love you as a very good friend now," it felt as though a piece not only of my heart, but of my soul had been instantaneously shattered.

My entire identity was intertwined in us, and I within him.

I was not the same girl who would spunkily start her own student organization and happily debate "the boys" on political issues and stand alone comfortably by myself. I had lost that version of myself in my hope to keep him and to keep us.

I had wanted so earnestly for Will to be mine always and for our lives to be "'til death do us part." I see now that it maybe wasn't always with the best of intentions. It wasn't that I didn't love him or had secret ulterior motives or anything like that. It was just that in becoming so wrapped up in one another, I had started to become so dependent on Will that I didn't know what it was that I liked about myself in the first place. This was startling to realize, even months after our relationship ended.

I had subconsciously chosen to allow my perspective to change, and for my own confidence to dip down along with it. It seemed now that it had all been for nothing. Will was lost, and I needed to be found.

CHAPTER 8

TESORO

———

Let me paint a broader picture of what my life looks like at home. The first thing you should know is that my mom and I have nicknames for most of the neighbors surrounding us.

There are "the Russians," our next-door neighbors—the husband, the wife, another woman, a grandmother. The truth is, we don't know how many people live there. What we do know is that they receive at least three Amazon prime packages a week.

On the other side of our townhouse is "Treekiller," who we now refer to as Toni, ever since she started knocking on our door with homemade empanadas. When I was younger, Toni was famous for calling the neighborhood association and asking them to chop down any trees in her townhouse's immediate vicinity. For some reason, the association always listened, chopping down three of the most beautiful trees surrounding our two townhouses.

Then of course, there was the infamous "Cat Man Do," who for years allowed his two cats to roam about our neighborhood freely. He was also infamous for wearing painfully tight biker shorts, no matter the season, no matter the weather.

And so, this was where I was raised and how I was raised.

Our nicknames for our neighbors were part of the language my mom and I created together, a part of the banter only the two of us will ever fully comprehend.

We've always lived in the same place. This neighborhood and my mom are the only home I have ever known.

My dad once lived here in this house with us, but I only have one memory of him here. At this point, most of me thinks the memory is based off a photograph.

~

In the photo, my father sits in our living room, freshly home from work (was he working at the time? I'm honestly not sure) and wears a white button up shirt and a nice pair of trousers. His brown bread beard and mustache are trimmed neatly, though not too neatly. He's overweight and jovial. Like a younger-appearing Santa Claus of sorts.

I don't know yet that he's an alcoholic.

At the time this picture was taken, I am still only two or three years old, sitting on the floor and looking up at my father on the couch, watching as he stares off into the distance. The sun frames his face perfectly from a distance, casting him in an almost heavenly glow, and all of a sudden, his eyes flash into a smile as he looks my way. His eyes are my eyes, but I don't know this yet either.

Other than this memory, or perhaps my own imagination, this home has only ever been our womanly coven for two.

Fond childhood memories involved nurturing my American Girl dolls and reading Nancy Drew books and going to the library with my mom on Saturdays. There was of course the baking and snuggling and tickling and laughing and tears.

For most of my childhood, we had a dog. My dad bought Sierra for my mom even though she didn't want a dog. He brought Sierra home on a Valentine's Day before I was born, my parents' wedding anniversary. After their later divorce, likely not long after this photo was taken, my dad would leave Sierra too. She would remain ours for better or worse forever.

Years later, I sat in my childhood bedroom, trying to hide from the memories of another man— this time, my first love, Will.

My hope had been to mourn the end of our relationship at home with my mom—to speak our own language for two without any reminders of a relationship I recently lost. For a while after Will and I broke up, I was scared to go back to Washington, DC, the city where we met, and where I slowly but surely became more independent.

For a while, I continued to feel nervous and anxious to see what my life would truly look like in DC without Will there. Or rather, there but not *there*. Would the memory of him—of us—linger forever at every familiar street corner? Could I ever return to certain restaurants or parks or places again? Would it always hurt? How would I interact with those mutual friends we shared together like a badge of honor?

Any greater sense of understanding, and any real acknowledgement of this grief was initially put off by the coronavirus pandemic and our two separate homecomings.

~

Almost a month into that first homecoming, my friend Gwenyth sent me a poem by a woman named Yesika Salgado. A Salvadoran American, Yesika frequently wrote about the heartbreak she endured and the women who uplifted her.

Gwenyth sent me the poem "Soltera" from her book *Tesoro*.

I read this poem for the first time right as the clock struck midnight on April 10th, exactly a month after that big breakup. I cried in bed, lying there in the dark, reading the poem repeatedly to myself until I my breathing returned to normal.

And then I began to smile.

"The women would pull out the tools / and fix it themselves," writes Selgado.

It was everything I had ever known put into words. It was the language my mother and I casually spoke, and the special camaraderie that only forms between women.

The poem reminded me of all the women who had raised me. Because while my mom does have four biological sisters, her close friends always proved to be my real aunts.

I've always wanted to write about my aunts, and the impact they've had on me and my ideas of being a woman. They each taught me about various paths towards fulfillment. These women, along with my mother, have shaped me like clay into the fledgling woman I am today.

Maybe they each have given me the tools I need to continue to try to be a woman in my own right. To fix myself whenever and however it may be necessary. As I grow, they continue to grow too. These are my aunts, my treasure. My *tesoro*.

~

My Aunt Shell has short and close-cropped dyed platinum blonde hair, and in my childhood visions, she always wears long-sleeved button up shirts. She is a mother and a grandmother and a former security guard and school janitor and manual laborer.

She is flawed and she is beautiful, and she once overcame a devastating divorce. I hear about it sometimes, in short snippets from my mother. They worked together at a pizza joint as teenagers, and through thick and thin have been friends ever since.

Like cream, my Aunt Shell rises to the top. Her voice is my childhood, coming out of the other end of the phone as my mother listens on for hours and hours, for the weeks and years and decades that make up both of our lives. I hear the name "Aunt Shell" from my mother's lips, and I am again five, ten, fifteen years old.

~

My Aunt Roomana came back into our lives when my mom was diagnosed with colon cancer. Or at least, this is how it appears to me. I don't remember having any memories of her beforehand. She is a mother, realtor, and autism advocate and raised her two boys all on her own. Oh, and that's true of my Aunt Shell too, but she raised two girls instead.

Aunt Roomana curses like a sailor and brings us samosas and homemade chicken tikka every time she visits our house. She is why I will permanently associate Indian food with comfort —the food I ate while mom was sick. Her belly laughs will warm your heart, just as they've warmed mine. Her spirit is contagious.

~

Aunt Rose is my godmother and also a mother of two boys. She has been married to her husband for a good long time now, but she's not the type of woman that has ever been defined by her relationship to a man.

Aunt Rose is my vision of fulfillment. She is a social worker in the middle-of-nowhere Pennsylvania, and she camps out with her girlfriends for a massive folk music festival every August. She is a hippie and a peacekeeper and a truth-teller. My Aunt Rose speaks her mind always—often gently, but when provoked, *she's provoked.*

I grew up watching these women—how they soared, how they failed, how they would at times disappoint themselves and each other. I watched their relationships with my mother blossom and fade at different points throughout their lives, but ultimately never break.

I grew up listening to every old story there ever was to tell. I noticed the shine still in their eyes, the wrinkles of experience that had slowly formed with age, and the red-hot banter and wit they each constantly kept about them. I saw familiarity and femininity. I saw some inkling of myself in them, and the person that I wanted myself to be.

I saw again the secret language that comes with age and treasured friendship.

Reading the poem "Soltera" that night, the pain of rejection and love gone to waste was still so fresh in my mind. The pain I felt from my breakup had its own pulsing heartbeat for a few months afterwards, and for a time it seemed to lodge itself into my spirit. It physically hurt for a long time, too. My mind was a dull throb with a repetitive feedback loop I worried would never go away.

But reading that poem, I thought of my aunts (somehow both figurative and literal) and all they had survived. All that they had taught me. They too must have felt this heartbreak and weariness at some point in their lives.

I felt a little less alone, picturing myself again as a child, each of them making separate visits to our tiny two-bedroom townhouse. Two middle-aged women with a beer each and an old war story from work or home to share with one another. A laugh or sigh of frustration, the glisten of a single tear even, never far beyond their reach.

I watched all these interactions as a child, teen, and young adult with wonderment and awe. Could I have this for myself and my own daughter one day?

Could these relationships—these friendships that struggled under the weight of time, arguments, divorces, death, addiction, diseases and more—could these relationships be worth so much more than the love that I just lost?

I thought, as I held myself closely under the covers that night, I thought that just maybe they might.

In my relationship, I had lost myself. In my grief, I had begun to find myself again. I have done this many times, over and over and over. The pain from this period reminded me so much of my mother's cancer and the sense of loss I had felt then.

But no matter what the situation may be, I have learned that my treasure is in the people that love and stick by every iteration of myself. The people who love and stand by me, despite any changes or mistakes that I may make.

I once believed with every fiber of my being that Will loved me unconditionally—that no matter what, to him I would always be a priority and a place to call home. While that belief has no truth behind it anymore, I believe that it once did.

I believe that I may find it again with some other man on some other day, but if I don't—I'll be just fine.

I have my treasures: my mother, my aunts, my friends. I have my "tesoro." And for now, I have my "soltera."

PART 2

COUNTRIES

CHAPTER 9

THE FIRST WAR OF ITALIAN INDEPENDENCE

———

I grew up watching Samantha Brown on the Travel Channel or watching *Eat, Pray, Love* with my mom, marveling at the thought of international travel and experiencing a world outside of my own. Together in our two-bedroom townhouse, my mom and I would develop an "us against the world" mentality that seemed to work in our favor as each of us grew older.

In college, I decided to study abroad in Italy, where my maternal great-grandparents emigrated from. Whereas some of my friends would go on to study in Paris or Prague, the decision to study in Italy felt natural to me.

This is where my people are from, I thought.

I had recently turned twenty when I first landed in Milan in September of 2019. I was deeply in love with my then-boyfriend Will, and even now, some five years after her initial diagnosis, overly concerned with my mother's health. The thought of a cancer recurrence caused me to panic at least once every week.

The decision to study abroad during the fall of my junior year had been a difficult one to make. I felt marked by the grief of leaving my mom and Will over 4,000 miles away and five hours behind in time.

I was worried that grief would encompass me in some way. In some ways it did.

In the final days leading up to that semester, I wondered if the happy bubble I had created within my relationships at home would permanently pop during that flight off to Milan. I wondered if live would be the same without me and if I would be wanted when I returned home.

In the end, I felt okay with what I believed to be my own perceived selfishness.

I felt exhilaration at the thought of my own dream finally coming true.

Landing at the Milan Malpensa airport, I could feel the tears gathering in the corners of my eyes as my plane began to touch down. Though my mom had never been to Italy herself, I imagined I was seeing Italy through her eyes and her parents' eyes.

All I could see as we touched down were the airport terminal and the expansive fields of green that surrounded it. Yet it felt different somehow. I felt home.

Everything around me was sure to bring a closer understanding of the culture and values that our family was built upon.

Here I was, here in *her* home. Here I was, for Millie.

~

That first afternoon, I met my host mother Lorenza and the rest of the family I'd be living with for the next three and a half months. Lorenza, Ettore, Gianpiero, Luca, Corrado and Cecilia. Three brothers and a sister! I hadn't slept much on either one of my two flights to Milan, but I still refused to sleep that first night before 9 p.m. It felt like a challenge to me to avoid jet lag and get my life here in Italy started on the right foot from the very beginning.

The language barrier between us quickly became evident during that first afternoon with Lorenza, as the two of us walked up and down the popular Milanese shopping district of Corso Buenos Aires. A mere few blocks away from Lorenza's family apartment, Corso Buenos Aires boasted an H&M and Lindt chocolate store that my friends and I would frequent for cheap purchases and free samples in the months to come. Not exactly the most Italian, but beloved by us, nonetheless.

"I took Italian lessons for four years in high school, but I don't remember too much now," I told Lorenza.

"Va bene! Sei molto bravo!" she said in response.

I tried not to grimace in embarrassment. I was constantly wishing that I knew more, could say more.

"Grazie," I said in reply, a nervous, small smile flitting across my face.

Though I'm sure I came off a bit harried and overwhelmed that first afternoon, Lorenza immediately took me in the way that all Italian mothers take young people in —like we are stray cats or dogs simply in need of extra love (and food).

She then taught me a lesson. It would be the first of many lessons I would learn while in Italy.

"The color—the color of the city is yellow," said Lorenza.

My favorite color, how about that?

Lorenza's apartment building, where I would live for the next several months, was painted with a faint and comforting glow synonymous with the Italian countryside and the hills of Tuscany. Yellow, golden yellow.

In the bustling and metropolitan city of Milan, yellow could be found in countless small details: in the color of the flowers lacing small apartment balconies, in the world-renowned clothing worn by both men and women on the street, in the small guzzled down shots of delicious limoncello, and at the sight of many of the city's well-worn buildings.

Lorenza explained to me that all this yellow had to do with the Austrian occupation of northern Italy during the First Italian War of Independence in the 1800s.

First Italian War of Independence, I thought.

The political history of Italy was not something I had learned about from my grandmother or any of my various American Italian language teachers.

What I remembered most from my first two years of high school Italian was that my Profe (teacher) thought that the perfect breakfast was toast with ricotta and honey. The only progress our small group of girls seemed to make throughout those first two years was conjugating the verbs "essere" and "andare" over and repeatedly until we thought our eyes would bug out.

Essere – "to be"

Io sono

Tu sei

Lui/lei e

Noi siamo

Voi siete

Loro sono

With that context in mind, I couldn't help but be struck by my own lack of knowledge about a country I had idolized and felt so connected to throughout my childhood.

The lack of knowledge that we have as Americans about the rest of the world was something I would become familiar with throughout my time in Europe, and something that I have not done a good job of remediating in the time since.

In writing this book, I've done my own research on Milan, Austria, and the color yellow—and the connection truly is worth noting.

According to one source, in 1815, the Congress of Vienna returned control of northern Italy to the Habsburgs of the Austrian Empire. Countless uprisings and attempts at an Italian revolution would take place throughout the decades that followed, until The Five Days of Milan, an 1848 uprising that finally forced the Austrian garrison to leave the city altogether.

But before the Austrian garrison could be forced out, the color of yellow had permeated throughout the city.

The flag of the Habsburg Monarchy consisted of two horizontal stripes of black and yellow, at one time likely flown highly and proudly throughout the overtaken city of Milan.

To me, yellow had already come to symbolize my own betterment, or at least a chance for growth.

Yellow was the color of my mom's old hospital socks, the socks I slipped onto her feet each night while during the day she endured chemotherapy. Yellow could also be found within the bright mustard yellow backpack I carried around everywhere throughout college and across Milan itself.

Above all else, and as silly as it sometimes felt, yellow constantly served me as a rudimentary symbol of hope.

It still does.

Of course, these were all loose connections to a color and a city I hardly knew. Finding yellow here, on my first day in Milan, felt as though it was some sort of validation—or even confirmation. For if even just a moment, everything around me felt as though it was falling into place.

Each morning throughout that semester, I would go to the gym I had paid an exorbitant amount of money to join throughout my stay in Milan (paying close to 200 euros for three months if we want to get specific about it).

Every morning, Lorenza would ask me: "Vado in palestra?" as I shuffled my way out her apartment door.

"Si, vado in palestra," I would smile back to her as I spoke with a half-chewed biscotti in the corner of my mouth.

After my approximately seven-minute walk over to the gym, I would force myself to go for a jog, listening to American pop music and running on treadmills where my distance was now measured in kilometers rather than miles.

My study abroad center was close to the center of the city, but my homestay apartment was in the neighborhood of Loreto, and I had to take the Milan metro every morning and afternoon in order to get to and from my classes.

My commute to class took about thirty minutes each way, the metro whizzing past stop after stop until finally we arrived, via the green line, at fermata di Sant'Ambrogio. I had despised the slowness and inconsistency of the DC metro throughout the past two years, and even further disliked my own lack of knowledge of the system itself.

In Milan, understanding the metro system became a necessity instantaneously, and by October I felt that I had mastered the green and red lines. I knew my local stops and I knew how to time the end of my last class with the next incoming metro train. I also knew no matter what happened, how to get myself back home.

Back in DC, Will and I would ride the metro together every so often for a date in the neighboring town of Alexandria, or to visit our friends in the NoMa neighborhood of the city.

At almost every stop along the way, Will would mimic the DC metro operator perfectly with his imitation of, "Next stop, doors closing."

Where some might find this annoying, I found it endearing.

In Milan, I would sometimes whisper to myself and think of him as I'd say to myself: "Prossima fermata, next stop."

Living in Milan inherently meant adjusting to a new schedule. Both my mom and Will would almost always be up for the morning around 10 or 11 a.m. my time, meaning 5 or 6 a.m. their time. My mornings often didn't feel real to me until I received a simple good morning text from either one of them.

At the same time, on other mornings I felt a little freer in my perceived solitude and answering their texts in the middle of my classes felt like a chore.

Getting used to life in Milan meant grappling with the fact that my existence had suddenly been splintered into two factions: here with my new friends and Italian family and there, back home. It felt similar to that first adjustment during my freshman year of college, when I had first moved to a city three hours away from home. But the significance of this intercontinental separation, this distance between us, would never truly die down in the months to come.

Soon enough, I began to make friends with the other students in my program. The first real friend I made was named Alyssa, a senior at Johns Hopkins, who was slightly intimidating in her sense of intellect and self-assuredness. I liked her instantly for those two qualities and for her willingness to explore the city. Within four or five days of the initial start of our program, the two of us planned a weekend trip to Prague. We barely knew each other and had no idea what traveling between European countries was like. Fortunately, it was one of the best decisions I made that semester.

Three of my close friends from college had spent their own semesters abroad in the bohemian Czech capital, and I had yearned to visit since. I wanted to try the dessert trdelnik, to visit Prague Castle and to see the beautiful glowing orange rooftops I had seen in the many, many pictures they had posted online.

Alyssa was quick to join in my excitement, and for that I was especially grateful.

With our quickly blossoming friendship, I had an instant sparring partner, someone who *got it* amongst a sea of partying-focused classmates, and Milan instantly felt a little bit more like home. Together, Alyssa and I would often go on long walks, sometimes with other students in our program, throughout Milan before our classes began to truly take off.

Alyssa and I sought to familiarize ourselves with various sections of the city, venturing past the beloved and beautiful Milanese Duomo, and to the Navigli district, to see the long stretches of canal-lined streets supposedly designed by Da Vinci and to devour yet another cone of delicious gelato.

Bacio, or chocolate hazelnut for me, strawberry for her.

On one of those first afternoons exploring the city together, a rainstorm came in unexpectedly. Alyssa had packed an umbrella, she was always armed with a duffle bag of all the essentials, while I had not. I remember huddling underneath her navy-blue umbrella together that afternoon, half exhilarated and half miserable, looking for the nearest metro station in a city we had yet to know, with a language we could hardly speak.

"What do we do now?" I said to her with a laugh as the rain started to pour down.

"We could walk around a little bit more, see how bad it gets?" she offered.

Together, we laughed and marveled and embraced the rain until we felt compelled to go our separate ways home. The moment felt idyllic and magical, the way that simply being in a foreign country seemed to cast a rose-colored lens over the everyday mundaneness of my average weekday in Milan.

It's weird now looking back at this time in my life, where the smallest of memories and details have become almost mythical simply due to their origin. The specific coffee cups used each morning in my homestay, the most popular types of biscotti found within our kitchen cupboard, the French bulldogs I spotted on the street, and the faces of the many patrons at my small gym are forever ingrained in my mind.

As my first few weeks in Italy continued to pass by, I began to pick up on some of the more common phrases customary to those living in Milan. I learned that saying the right thing, or at least attempting to speak Italian, could get you extremely far in terms of restaurant service or customer service in general.

I learned the saying "Buona giornata!" from my abroad program Community Assistant, Bea.

"It means, 'have a good day,'" said Bea. "And we say it a lot when we're leaving a store."

Saying the phrase often meant a quick smile from Italian shopkeepers. I. As is the case here in the United States, my favorite places in the world to wander around tend to be bookstores and coffee shops.

With time, as "Buona giornata," "Grazie mille" and a million other small Italian phrases made their way into my vernacular—my daily interactions with Italians became much more interesting.

Throughout my three and a half months of living in Milan, I told myself that while I was there— learning the culture, learning the language, traveling as much as possible— I could also learn to become a more observant person. Someone quieter, someone who could take a moment to breathe rather make the very most out of every moment.

Instead of quieting myself and my anxieties down to observe, I often quieted most of my feelings entirely.

After those first few weeks in Italy, the allure of yellow and mysticism of living somewhere new quickly began to fade.

What would happen next?

Who would I become next?

I had yet to find out.

CHAPTER 10

YOU, ME, SICILY

———

The minute we stepped off our plane in Catania, Sicily it felt as though we had truly entered an entirely different part of the world. Palm trees swayed in the distance, their fronds looking more relaxed than frantic. At the same time, the sky was a crisp cerulean blue, more at peace than I had ever seen it before.

Yet, in Italy, even a century and a half after the country's reunification, there were still blatant divides and hostilities between the north and the south.

I remember my host family looking slightly disappointed when I had first explained to them, "Mia nonna era Siciliana." No northern Italian blood was coursing through my veins, and I had been raised to be proud of my heritage.

My grandmother, Mildred Maita Edmondson was born in 1925 in Passaic, New Jersey. She was the youngest of six sisters, born of Italian immigrants. My mother was her youngest daughter, and I was her youngest granddaughter.

Together, my grandmother and her sisters were raised to be proper Sicilians; their parents emigrated from the island before settling in the United States. Family is everything to Sicilians, along with finishing everything on your plate, and stoking passions and tempers that often flared on a dime.

My family, their hearts were filled with gold, anchovies, and ricotta cheese.

My grandmother went on to have six children of her own, four girls, including my mother, and two boys. In 1959, when my mother was two years old, her father died in a fatal car accident where they had lived in Charleston, South Carolina. I don't know any of the specifics of the accident itself, and I doubt that my mother really does either. What I do know is that my maternal grandmother was left to raise six children on her own at a time when women were barely making their way into the workforce.

Ironically, when her husband died, my grandmother didn't know how to drive.

Instead of falling apart at the stress of it all or quickly remarrying a man she didn't love, my grandmother took her six children and moved back up north to be closer to her family. She secured a job working at McGuire Air Force Base in New Jersey.

Mildred Edmondson was a tour de force: a devoted mother, an avid fan of Frank Sinatra, and more than anything, a Sicilian with deep roots.

My mother and her siblings were indoctrinated as kids with a twentieth century understanding of what it means to be an Italian American. There were big family Sunday dinners with spaghetti and meatballs, arguments across the dinner table, a distinctive love of biscotti, and all other Italian pastries, and finally—an affinity for inappropriate Italian hand gestures.

~

In late September, the city of Catania was balmy and beautiful—an ambience that made the ancient city immediately feel like a dreamed-of tropical oasis, readily preferred over the often-stifling city of Milan. The air felt crisper here in Sicily—cleaner, infused with greater stillness. As our group of students sheepishly followed our designated chaperones, I forced myself to be diligent in mentally recording our every move. I knew I would want to relay every detail of this trip to my mother back home.

My mother. I didn't realize the ache I would feel going on this trip without her.

But here I was, *home*. I knew that everything that my grandmother and mother had done had led to this opportunity, to this very moment. My chest couldn't help but surge with pride.

I had made it back.

We had made it back.

By that next afternoon in Catania, our group of students was ready to explore Mount Etna and the surrounding area. It barely registered to me at first that we were on our way to visit an active volcano, and once there, the sight before me didn't meet the dramatic expectations I had set in my mind.

For some reason, in my head, I had imagined our visit to have the imagery of a dystopian novel or Dwayne "The Rock" Johnson adventure movie, yet the whole ordeal was quite calm. There was no boiling lava threatening to bubble over a volcano's crater and consume us all. Rather, due to the high elevation, it was even chilly.

Together, with my friends Alyssa and Katherine, we took turns taking pictures as we stared in awe at the ash, the dark volcanic rock, and the seemingly new world around us.

I collected a few of the larger rocks in my pocket as keepsakes, with the sudden weight of feeling physically on top of the world.

Reveling in a certain kind of transcendence, I remember feeling more alive in that moment than I had at any time before.

It was the discovery of a newfound love, of my own perceived limitlessness, with Alyssa calling ahead of me: "climb up this slope with me!"

"Hold on, wait, I'm coming!" I yelled up to her with a laugh, my sneakers slipping a little on the volcano's gravel.

It felt good to feel so tall.

It was in that short thirty minutes or so at Mount Etna that my feeling of belonging to Sicily, this island where my ancestors had once lived really began to sink in.

It wasn't a learned feeling or sense of home, as I had previously felt in DC or would later feel that semester in Milan.

Rather, this sense of belonging was innate, and maybe because of the way I had been raised, it felt deserved. Sicily had unlocked a kind of familial confidence and love buried deep inside of me, and that realization itself was priceless.

I belonged here in Sicily, and I never wanted to leave.

I noticed a sense of ancestral validation I felt connected to my love of seafood as our group of students visited an outdoor market. That morning, we each took turns posing with one Sicilian man and the octopus he was desperately trying to sell. I had grown up eating fish at least once a week with my mother from our local farmer's market. We joked that the owner of the little seafood joint was my mother's "husband," imagining a dream world where we'd have fresh seafood at our disposal whenever we wanted it.

While my friends were grossed out by the sights and smells surrounding us at the market that day, to me it felt like coming home. I smiled as if every Sicilian knew me. I smiled as if I knew them.

~

Later that afternoon, the calm and comforting waves of the Mediterranean Sea would remind me of all I had kept bottled within me, the doubts and anxieties I had brought with me to Italy, and also on this trip.

Together, my friends and I swam out into the sea, giggling and laughing, in complete amazement at the water's aqua translucence and dazzling warmth.

That afternoon, I felt free. Rather, I felt carefree.

It was a feeling that I hadn't truly felt in a very long time. I didn't realize how much I had been holding onto, until for a few moments, I decided to let it go.

I would remember that freeing feeling in the Mediterranean throughout those next few months in Italy, when the loneliness and anxiety about my relationships back home would begin to sink in again. By remembering those few moments of peace, I would be granted a few moments of relief.

I believed and repeated to myself that if I could just slow down my breathing and take my mind back to those waters, maybe I could feel that release again.

~

For our last stop in Sicily, my classmates and I visited the tiny town of Taormina, a UNESCO World Heritage Site rich with the history of its famed Teatro Greco. Its cobblestone streets and promise of ancient ruins excited all of us, even after what felt like one of the longest days imaginable. After an afternoon of relishing the late summer sun as we swam in the Mediterranean, we all were glad the sky had turned overcast.

Here at the Teatro Greco, Alyssa and I broke away from the rest of our group to walk around by ourselves, always within listening range of the rest of our group.

As we navigated the site without a tour guide, we were quicker to spot the view below us. From our now higher vantage point amongst the ancient ruins, the view of the Mediterranean below us was startling. To fall off one of Taormina's many towering cliffs would certainly mean death. The threat of the fall, and the danger of the sea below us was mesmerizingly beautiful.

The knowledge that we had only swam in the sea ourselves just hours before made the view even more surreal.

I reveled in the fact that I still reeked of sea water beneath the tank top and jean shorts I had hastily thrown over my still-damp bathing suit. An avid lover of the water since birth, I craved the messiness of sandy and salt-drenched hair.

Standing there, reveling in my absolute brininess, I felt closer to my grandmother here in Sicily than I ever had before.

~

Over a year later now, I continue to miss that fall's quick, three-day trip to Sicily. On any given day, I find myself trying to draw upon the strength of my grandmother, that woman who raised six children on her own, and the tenacity, humor, and sheer grit she put into everything she did. In visiting

Sicily, in coming home, I felt that maybe I had finally become the granddaughter she could truly be proud of.

Maybe I was someone she would have wanted to know.

Throughout my childhood, I had tied my own understanding of strength so much to what my grandmother and my mother had both overcome in their lives, that any perceived strength of my own could only pale in comparison.

Now twenty-one, I struggled to believe that I might possess that same strength. I struggled to imagine myself coming out on the other side of divorce, of death, of cancer or of such extreme pain in the way that they had.

I realized in Sicily that I had my own story worthy of telling, and that familial, feminine strength I had been raised with didn't have to be a sign of my own struggle to come, or of traits that I was destined to emulate with time.

I understood that I could pay homage to my family while still working to find myself individually.

I understood that while my family wasn't perfect, they had done the best they could. The best I could was all I could offer in the end, too.

And then I took in a deep breath and let my bundled-up worries spill out.

The sea still glinting in the sun below me, my newfound sense of discovery felt revelatory and undoubtedly ancestral in nature. I knew what I needed to do to further my own growth. I knew that it was time I write my story.

CHAPTER 11

HALLOWEEN NIGHT

———

"Have a mixed drink?" said Ricardo, flirtatiously, and with a smile.

Unlike many of the names included throughout this book, Ricardo is neither a person's true name nor an outright pseudonym. The fact is, I don't remember the name of my host brother's friend, the one I'd developed the most innocent of crushes on.

"Sure, I'll have a drink," I sheepishly responded with a smile.

It was Halloween night and my host brother, Corrado, had invited me to join him and his friends for a Halloween party. I had balked at his initial invitation, having long preferred throughout my semester abroad to sit at home doing homework or FaceTime my then-boyfriend Will.

And speaking of Will, I hadn't been drinking for months at this point. Months earlier, Will had decided to completely stop drinking alcohol altogether.

The two of us shared similar absentee, alcoholic, asshole dads (the 3 As),so I immediately understood his decision. In a semi-conscious choice of solidarity, I had essentially stopped drinking too.

Yet now there was Ricardo, standing in front of me, asking if I wanted a drink.

I found that I did.

"So, I listened to the Wilco? The band you told me about," said Ricardo over the noise of the party.

I felt my face light up. My favorite band, something I had mentioned in passing during a brief meeting some weeks earlier.

"What did you think of them?" I asked in earnest.

"Very good, very good," said Ricardo. I watched his hands. I thought of Will and felt myself shrink back into myself.

My smile had softly melted in an instant, remembering how trapped our relationship could make me feel at times. How much I was under Will's thumb.

~

Earlier in the night, Corrado had stood tall and gaunt before me, his frame casting a shadow that engulfed us both. My favorite of my three Italian host brothers, Corrado was the friendliest person I had ever met—constantly welcoming me on outings with his circle of friends and reassuring me that my presence never felt awkward. If anything, I sometimes made myself feel that way, even if there never was any reason to.

"You see Liz, they are having a Halloween party at the university tonight and I think you should come!"

Corrado had looked at me expectantly, his smile and enthusiasm almost contagious. I felt myself fill with dread.

A few hours later, when I finally ran down the apartment's short spiral staircase to tell Corrado the good news, "I'm coming!", a wide, boyish grin quickly spread across his face.

"Oh, that's wonderful Liz, I'm so excited for you to come!"

What he didn't know was that for a good hour or so beforehand, I had agonized over my decision. To go out drinking with a bunch of Italians at the time felt like some sort of betrayal—initially, I thought, to the idea of sobriety I had built with Will. It was only later I would realize that it was a betrayal to that carefully crafted version of myself.

When I asked Corrado how we would be getting to this party, assuming that we would be taking the Milan metro, he surprised me again.

"We will take the bikes!"

The bikes? I could feel apprehension sneak back up again.

"Corrado, I don't have a bike and um, to be honest I'm not the most confident bike rider in general."

"This is no problem Liz, no problem."

I can still hear his distinctive, comforting Milanese accent saying "no problem" to me now.

As the two of us bundled up in a few layers of coats and scarves it had gotten surprisingly cold in Milan by the last week of October—my host brother showed me how my lack of bike-riding skills was "no problem."

As Corrado dug out his bike, I made a mental note that my host family didn't even own enough bicycles for me to steer one of my own.

A moment later, I gave Corrado an incredulous look that seemed to say: "So...what's the plan?"

"I'll make a seat, you see, right here," said Corrado, pointing to a small wire frame attached to the back of his bicycle seat, and now hanging precariously off the bike's back wheel.

"I'm going to sit on that?" I asked, failing to hide my complete shock.

I had already been enough of a pain in the ass with my indecision about the party earlier. But this? I thought at this rate when people advised their friends to "live a little" it should be emphasized that it was a little, and not a *lot*.

But sure enough, I scooted my butt onto that tiny make-shift seat and clung onto Corrado for dear life, as we quickly took off into the darkened streets of Milan. Feeling the biting cold, the wind whipping through my hair, and still slightly worried for our collective safety—I felt myself come alive floating past the familiar shops lining Corso Buenos Aires.

There was the Italian McDonald's and five different ATM machines and gelato shops and Intimissimi lingerie shop I passed by almost daily. We met Corrado's girlfriend Milli and a few others about halfway to the party, and after a quick conversation, I was entrusted with transporting three mas-sive Peroni-style bottles of beer within a thinly veiled plastic grocery bag.

Viva la birra!

So, again clutching onto Corrado for dear life, I now bal-anced three massive glass bottles of beer in my lap, nervous for the sudden jolt that would come with every stop light but exhilarated at the new life I found myself living. A life where I decided outside of my comfort zone. Without the protection and control of Will. Without the limitations I afforded myself.

It was a fleeting few moments for me, and me alone. I hadn't felt myself enjoy that type of freedom in far too long.

Corrado and I biked past the Milanese Duomo that Halloween night. The massive gothic spires of the famous cathedral reflected the light of the moon from above and cast everything in a silvery, hushed glow. I found myself dazzled by the beauty in the motion of it all, the barely held glances with what lay before us as we whizzed past sights now unfamiliar in the dark.

Together, bundled up and hanging on for dear life to Corrado's bicycle, it felt as though we were floating through the wind. The tips of my ears turned pink with the cold and my fingertips began to go numb. Groggy and exhilarated all at once, I felt my heart soar.

I took a moment to observe the inviting yet curious details of the city that surrounded me—appreciating Milan in a way I had never seemed to before. I felt in a way, more forgiving towards myself in that moment too.

Electricity and adrenaline ran through my veins as my legs ached through block after block. Not pedaling in any way, I had to use my quad muscles to keep my legs in a permanent hover off the ground in order to prevent Corrado's bike from stopping.

My eyes became blurry with tears the way they often do when the wind strikes them fiercely, but a part of me wanted to cry for other reasons. I didn't realize how much I had been suffocating myself until this moment.

It was the first time in a very long time that I felt free. Even if only temporarily, I had watched myself rediscover my own independence, slowly emerging as a purer and more unadulterated version of myself.

I felt myself changing and I felt that desire to change even more bubbling beneath the surface. Tired of hiding behind a more agreeable and complacent version of myself, I wanted to be fully of my own sound mind and body again—trusting in myself before anybody else.

Watching as my icy breath floated into the air that cold October night, I felt something in me shift for the better.

CHAPTER 12

TEN P.M. IN PARIS

After a quick glance at my surroundings, noting the dispositions of the people that sat nearby, I carefully sat down and pressed my fingers to the keys.

Do re mi fa so la ti do

C D E F G A B C

A few weeks after that Halloween night in Milan, I found myself in Paris. Or rather, I found myself leaving Paris, in the Charles de Gaulle airport. I came to Paris for the weekend to visit my friend Grace, who at the time was more of a friend of a friend rather than my friend alone. By the time the weekend ended, we had formed a connection I believed would stand the test of time, of distance, and the sporadic nature of our many check-ins with one another that would follow.

Paris!

I was excited not by the fashion or romance of the city, but the idea of a bohemian and cosmopolitan lifestyle, of walking the city streets where the "Lost Generation" of Hemingway and Gertrude Stein had come to congregate, host salons, and spread their own fantastical ideas.

The itch to write and describe my experiences as I understood them had long been within me, and the idea that Paris was a hunting ground or even a mecca for doing so, left me thrilled.

I turned my attention back to the piano. Seeing that it was mid-November, I chose to play a Christmas song. Or, a non-Christmas-y, Christmas song.

After a quick google, I was able to pull up the sheet music. Sitting there, at a red baby grand piano in the middle of the Charles de Gaulle airport, I began to play Joni Mitchell's "River," on the piano.

~

By the time the Parisian metro pulled into my destination stop that Thursday night, I was absolutely famished. It was also 10:30 p.m. and I was desperate to find Grace and her hostel. Travelling often felt like a leapfrog voyage towards safety, constantly searching for one self-designated "safe zone" after another.

That night, as I walked through Paris in the dark, I sought the familiar solace of Oreos.

Snagging myself a six pack of cookies, I confidently strode my way out of the underground and onto the streets of Paris, plunging myself into a street lit sidewalk just along the Seine.

What I noticed first was the yellow.

Yellow was everywhere and in everything—a glow cast by streetlights that dotted the street along the Seine with every block I walked towards Grace. The light was enough for me to still catch my reflection in the river below me, bundled up in a winter coat, my own yellow backpack packed to the brim, its straps tucked in cautiously under my arms.

In the end, I was the night's only witness.

It was a moment, like so many other moments through-out my travels, of sheer gratitude. Noticing my own sense of gratitude, I realized, was often when I felt best. It felt like a complete gift to know that this moment by the Seine would forever characterize the first moments of my trip to Paris. It felt like an even greater gift to know that this stillness, this welcoming glow on a cold night in a foreign city, belonged only to me.

~

"Hello, hello, hello!" exclaimed Grace.

"Hi, it's so, so good to see you!" I nearly shouted back.

Throughout our short weekend in Paris together, Grace and I would talk, and talk, and *talk*.

I quickly learned how Grace could bring out the best in me, not only in the way she listened to my ideas about writing, but in the way she made me feel so appreciated and seen for who I am.

As much as I was still grateful and eager to go on weekend adventures, do well in my classes, apply to spring internships, and do everything else I did to occupy my time abroad—my loneliness was becoming a weight harder to bear on my own.

While my classmate Alyssa was a quick confidant and friend, I knew that spending all of our time together would drive both of us insane. And at times I did find myself star-tlingly more okay on my own, happy with more time to draw my attention towards what I was writing, both for my classes and for my own pleasure.

"Let me tell you about another idea I have," said Grace in between laughs.

"Okay, you go, then I'll go, then you go again. And then more hot chocolate!" I replied.

It was throughout those conversations with Grace that I realized something. While I had always been more passionate about writing than anything else, I hadn't felt any true confidence in my own writing skill in years.

Who would want to listen or read my work?

"Well, I would love to read your book," said Grace one afternoon.

"Whatever that might be, whenever it rightfully gets published."

She looked at me decisively, with not a doubt in her eye.

Her confidence in me was illuminating.

As we strolled through the windy streets of Paris that November weekend, Grace listened as I told her about my latest novel idea: a fictionalized ancestral history about my maternal great-grandmother moving from Sicily to Milan in the early twentieth century and her journey to the United States to create a better life for herself. The American dream.

My family's American dream.

The book would be my idealized, Italian, feminist version of events—rooted in my own powerful relationships with my mother and grandmother. I loved the idea in theory, and the homage that it would serve, but inspiration ran dry whenever I sat down to write.

Writing dialogue especially doesn't come naturally to me. How do people speak? What would that person have said, in 1919, in Northern Italy, but in English? Even as I told her that my story was likely going nowhere, Grace listened to me drone on and on about my idea with an ever brighter smile on her face.

"That's an incredible idea, Liz!" she practically gasped with enthusiasm.

"I can tell that this means a lot to you, and I bet it'll mean a lot to your mom too. I've actually been writing something that's sort of similar. Or, at least related to my family, my grandfather in particular," Grace explained.

The thing is, I don't remember ever telling my mom about that initial book idea. My plan was to write something more considerable, more worthy of showing by the time I landed back home at Philly International Airport—and then I would tell her.

"Here is my book about grand mom, inspired by grand mom and by you!" I would say.

It would be the ultimate souvenir, and I had already etched the expected look of pride on her face deep within my mind.

Only, I couldn't bring myself to write it.

Eventually, that story ran dry and ultimately crumpled into yet another one of the countless failed attempts at writing my first book. But Grace had seen that initial passion in me and chose to validate it.

For my part, I tried to provide her with the same kindness and attentiveness that she granted me.

In Paris, she told me about some of her previous writing projects, of short stories she wrote and tried to get published, and about the thesis on international affairs she was begging her academic advisors to let her write in the form of a screenplay.

Grace spoke with unadulterated excitement, as if writing itself was more than just an act, but a greater extension of herself that spread slowly from her brain to her fingertips clacking on the keyboard. Writing as a form of electricity, or as a life force, or as the grounds for lifelong friendship.

~

Mostly though, we really would just walk and talk in the same select city blocks for hours on end. The frigid wind bit back behind the tips of my ears until I gave in to buying an overpriced powder blue winter hat at a nearby tourist stand, fuzzy on the inside and with the Eiffel Tower proudly displayed on the outside.

Together, Grace and I would devour many of France's delicious delicacies—stuffing our faces with crepes and croissants, the indulgence feeling almost transformative on its own. The taste of a croissant melting in my mouth, with almonds encrusted on top like a perfectly bejeweled crown. The afternoon remnants of that morning's baked goods within a small bakery on the Ile Saint Louis.

~

I listened to Joni sing in my mind as I struggled to eke out the right notes to the chords once so familiar to me.

"Gate A24 to Milan Malpensa Airport," announced a robotic female voice over the airport loudspeaker in French-accented English.

To my surprise, the people surrounding me gave me a small round of applause, as we all shyly flashed smiles one another's way.

It was my time to go.

Yet thanks to Grace, I also knew it was my time to write.

CHAPTER 13

ROMA CITTÀ APERTA

I rolled out of my bed and hurriedly put on the pair of jeans and sweater I had set out for myself the night before.

Shoes?

Check.

Dab of mascara and foundation under my eyes?

Check and check.

I reached for the tan overcoat I bought myself earlier that week over on Corso Buenos Aires, arming myself with an umbrella and my purse before hurriedly making my way out the door.

I scampered my way over in the dark to Stazione Centrale, where I would catch my train that morning to Rome.

Rome in a single day. Exactly what they tell you *not* to do.

A day would grant me a single pious glance at the city, and the Vatican that formed my childhood beliefs.

From Milan, it would take about three hours to get there and three hours back—my journey requiring the highest of high-speed trains. It was just about 5:30 a.m. when my train to Rome was scheduled to set off, and as I shuffled in my seat, I tried to force myself to rest, ultimately to no avail.

Still in the final semi-stillness of morning, I found myself eager to embark on today's adventure.

~

Once my train safely arrived, I rushed from Rome's Stazione Termini to Panificio Pasticceria Roscioni—a bakery I had found in my beloved travel guidebook—and ordered myself a warm *sfoglie romane*, this beautiful, giant, flakey pastry with a layer of gooey apricot marmellata, topped with a dusting of powdered sugar.

If you couldn't tell at this point, I firmly believe that embracing the food in any region is the ultimate experience of life, and of culture. In all honesty, I could probably write a whole separate novel simply on Italian pasticcerias alone.

I remember feeling self-conscious, sitting there eating this pastry all by myself. In my two and half months of studying abroad, I had never dared to travel alone before. I wondered what the bakery owner and his patrons thought of me, this clearly American girl sitting on a small stool by herself—pretending to be cool and confident as she wolfs down a massive pastry for breakfast.

Will I go the entire day without talking to anyone?
What will that feel like?
What are mom and Will doing back home?
You've got this, it's one day. Shut up, shut up, shut up.

I felt sheepish sitting there, but I ultimately felt happy. I had a limited set of hours to explore one of the most famous cities in the world. In my journey towards finding my own independence again, travelling alone would have to be a necessary and fruitful test.

I had come to Rome to rediscover my faith, and in turn, hopefully rediscover my sense of self.

~

In the Italian cinema course I took that semester, we recently watched *Roma Città Aperta,* a neorealistic Rossellini film depicting the city during its occupation by the Germans in World War II. The film's heart is in the moral, political, and theological questions it poses to its viewers within the wake of pure devastation. How to forgive, how to live, how to survive in one's landscape?

The character I clung to most was Don Pietro Pellegrini, a partisan Catholic priest serving as a member of the Resistance, an underground coalition of Italians fighting against their Fascist counterparts and the Nazis that overtook their country.

With struggle after struggle, Don Pietro never gives up on his faith or his fellow man—even when giving his colleagues over to the Fascists may mean saving his own life.

When Pina, the film's tragic heroine, asks the priest how he continues to pray to God, and forgive the very individuals that have destroyed their lives completely, Don Pietro responds:

"So many people ask me that: 'Doesn't Christ see us?' But are we sure we haven't deserved this scourge? Are we sure we've always lived according to the Lord's laws? People never think of changing their ways, but when the piper must be paid, they despair and ask, 'Doesn't the Lord see us? Doesn't he take pity on us?' Yes, he does, but we have so much to be forgiven for, and for that we must pray and forgive many things."

This scene, portraying a sort of fatherly guidance and the idea of a deeper morality still within the priesthood gripped me throughout the day I spent in Rome. Long ago, I had stopped believing in any spiritual superiority that the clergy may have—especially to that of priests, due to the various scandals that had plagued my Catholic upbringing.

I felt a disdain and disregard for most formal arbiters of religion due to the pedophilia and abuse I watched scourge my faith from news station to news station, from pew to pulpit. I trusted and admired the nuns that ran my high school for the most part, but a sense of trepidation and distrust remained in my heart.

The sincere depiction of a good priest—"What makes a good man?"—embodied by Don Pietro Pellegrini did nothing to squash that mistrust, but all the same it gave me a renewed belief in the tenets of my faith itself.

It gave me renewed hope in the idea of forgiveness and humility not for lack of self-regard, but to fulfill an ultimately higher calling.

~

After a quick trip to the Colosseum (I wasn't a huge fan), I started to make my way towards Vatican City. Once there, the line to enter St. Peter's Basilica was decidedly hard to miss—a massive, serpent-like body of people stood before me in the cold, all waiting their turn to gawk and stare and pay their respects.

It was a cloudy day in Rome, and every one of us waiting in that line feared that the sky would open at any moment.

After those first few minutes of waiting, I noticed three girls in line in front of me—right about my age, talking excitedly amongst themselves in distinctly European-accented English. Though I had enjoyed the solitude of my morning and afternoon, my instinct is always to befriend.

I took a step forward.

"Hi," I said with a smile. "I couldn't help but hear that the three of you are in university too?"

I quickly learned that all three of these girls were university students like me, doing the European Erasmus version of study abroad within the European Union. All three were studying in Bergamo for the semester, a smaller city just north of Milan. One girl originated from Russia, another Austria, and the third girl was from the Netherlands.

Together, practically huddling in the ever-so-slow moving line to enter the basilica, we swapped stories of our differing lives growing up in our varying countries, discussing how we each felt about Northern Italy.

After what felt like a small eternity, but was only a little over an hour, the four of us were finally granted entry inside— at last entering the basilica for ourselves.

Once I stood there in the grand foyer of the Christian world's most beloved church, I remember thinking about Pope Francis and simply marveling at the thought of—*I'm standing where our Pope once stood. Where he'll come back and make announcements and stand again.*

I remember taking and sending pictures to my mom and to Will, as I did everywhere I went, and found myself amazed whenever I looked up.

Gazing up towards the high vaulted ceilings, it took me a minute to notice the delicately painted cherubs and saints, along with scenes from the Bible etched with care upon the highest rafters of the holiest of Catholic basilicas. There was an almost transcendent and relic-like quality to the gold used throughout each depiction, to the type of splendor that could inspire a sense of awe and trepidation in almost anyone, believer or nonbeliever.

Upon entry, our newly minted group of four stuck together for the most part, casually looking out for one another as we all perused and remained within relatively the same area. Quickly though, and to my later regret, my own curiosity urged me to move forward, to stay in constant motion and see more, *do more* in Rome before my train-mandated timer ran out and it was suddenly too late.

I wanted to whisper a quick goodbye to the three of those girls, or maybe even exchange phone numbers, but at that point in the afternoon, we were each seated a small distance apart inside one of the Basilica's smaller sacristy rooms reserved for reflection and adoration.

No talking was allowed within this sacred space, and in my mind, there was not a minute to spare.

I sheepishly worked my way out of the pew I was sitting in and made eye contact with each of them, giving a small smile and wave of goodbye as I made my way toward the door.

Moving on to other parts of the Basilica, I felt instant regret. I wasn't enjoying some profound moment of faith but felt rather the soft and persistent knocking of my own disappointment in myself.

It was true—I didn't really owe anything to three European college girls I met just an hour before, but in my eyes they deserved a real goodbye instead of my casual slip away.

I wanted the three of them to know that they mattered to me, and that they had made my solitary day feel more purposeful, less lonely, more substantial in sharing a part of it with them.

As I continued to walk throughout the chapel, I kept casting looks behind my shoulder, hoping that I would spot one of them in the distance behind me, but it was no use.

The onslaught of tourists and faithful now rushed in wave after wave—flashing their cameras, bowing their heads and grasping their rosary beads in tandem.

There would be no more looking back.

~

The final, and most notable stop of my quick trip was a short distance away at the Vatican Museums. Across Vatican City, signs pointed in its direction: Sistine Chapel here! Turn right in 400 meters! You can make it!

I wasn't particularly interested in visiting the museum. Rather, I was excited about checking off another item from my list.

My intentions were hurried, and I was flushed, and at this point in the day—emotionally and physically tired—simply ready to be indoors in another "safe zone." The museum was expected to close in less than an hour when I finally found my way to the top of the queue.

If I was even lucky enough to get in at all, I would have to make a mad dash to whichever room housed Michelangelo's most beloved work of art and just consider myself lucky. I felt unnervingly anxious. I was against the clock, and an uneasy yet smiling sort of adrenaline begun to course through my body.

Once inside, and with little time to spare, I paid the quick euro admission price and began speeding my way through exhibit after exhibit, in a desperate search to find that overwhelming claim to fame.

I sped past exquisite murals, floor to ceiling acrylic details, and centuries of art documenting the faith I identified with for so long.

If I had stopped to really think about it, I would have easily enjoyed the contents of the Vatican Museums much more than that of St. Peter's Basilica. But for the most part, I didn't give myself the chance.

It was only a short time later, after brushing past fellow tourists in room after room, that I noticed the time on my phone was 4:01 p.m. It was past the designated closing time, and no guards or museum officials seemed to be in any rush to kick us museumgoers out.

A sense of calm began to spread through me, releasing the tension I had stored up within my body throughout the day.

I felt my breath let out in a hitch, unaware that I had been holding it in the whole time.

The room in which I found myself was jaw-droppingly golden in all respects, from floor to ceiling. This was the room I'd been waiting for all along.

I felt personally enveloped in the color yellow as I stood there looking all around me.

The sheer amount of gold cast the entire room in a soft glow around me, as I finally tucked my phone and my fears back into my pocket. I was mesmerized by the familiarly carved depictions of religious figures. I was moved by the deeply held beauty and comfort this room brought out in me. I was a small child again, listening to the biblical parables I had become so accustomed to: the prodigal son, the loaves and the fishes, the coin and the sheep.

Both tears and a smile of transcendent happiness changed the entire nature of my face in just a few quick moments.

I was both home and so far away from home all at once.

Everything was yellow and everything was contingent on light.

I quickly took a picture of my surroundings, assuming that this must be the Sistine Chapel, because I had forgotten what the actual Sistine Chapel looked like. I couldn't imagine anything in this world—much less within this museum—being more beautiful than the gold and light and faith before me.

A quick Google search quickly proved my assumptions wrong, but I still felt the significance and weight behind the few minutes I spent in that room. That room in the Vatican Museum had been the call to faith of which I was desperately searching.

The feeling of peace that so instantly overcame me had been inertly spiritual—something I knew to be truth deep in my heart and in my gut. For a while afterward that afternoon, I felt a humility and reverence I didn't know I had within me. I will remember that feeling always.

It turns out, this room is called The Maps Hall or *Galleria delle Carte Geografiche*. As travel writer, Elyssa Bernard explains in her blog *Rome Wise*:

"The Gallery of Maps contains the largest collection of geographical paintings ever created. These wall-sized maps depict Italy and Italian provinces and were commissioned by Pope Gregory XIII in the 16th century. These maps, based on drawings by the Dominican Monk Ignazio Danti, are amazingly accurate for being made in the 1500's! The maps are really well-detailed, showing mountain ranges and even boats in the water, but they are also somewhat whimsical, containing fantastic sea creatures and even Neptune, the Roman god of the sea."

Maybe, whether I had known it or not, my own desire to travel and look outside of myself had brought me back to my faith. Or maybe it was simply the grandiose beauty of that *Galleria delle Carte Geografiche* ceiling.

Whatever it was, I still remain thankful.

I still remain now, just a little bit changed for the better.

CHAPTER 14

LISBON

"Let's have faith and be grateful." I whispered to Gwenyth as the two of us stood side by side in the Portuguese forest that surrounded us.

A long-legged, intuitive, West Coast girl, I was dazzled by my friend Gwyneth's quiet wisdom and humorous preference of rolling her eyes at any perceived indiscretion. At the same time, there was a sense of calm about her that I admired greatly. Together, the two of us now stood in the forests of Sintra, Portugal, waiting for two of our other friends to come back from the short climbing excursion they had gone on without us.

"Okay," Gwenyth nodded. "I can work with having faith and being grateful." We both laughed.

Our trip to Sintra, and to the city of Lisbon, Portugal in general, marked the last weekend adventure of our semester abroad, and had so far been plagued with miseries both in and out of our collective control. Together with our other friends Alyssa and Alice, the four of us had spent the previous night fighting over which restaurants to eat at, with rising tensions over who had falsely criticized who. That night at dinner, I would cry over the world's worst piece of cod fish, spitting bones out into a napkin with every other chew.

It will be years before I ever eat a piece of cod again.

The rest of that Friday had gone relatively well. That afternoon, I tried a pastel de nata, the beloved egg tart pastry of Portugal that my host mom back in Italy, Lorenza, fawned over the entire week leading up to my trip.

"Please, if you can, bring me one back!"

I didn't know how I would transport this delicate pastry through airport security, my flight and the bus ride it would take me to get home, but in the end, I was able to do it.

Earlier that Friday, my friends and I each gushed over Lisbon's signature tilework, hand-painted designs depicting bright blues and oranges and yellows, while we gawked at the towering Torre de Belém that jutted out into the sea. Climbing up to the tippy top of the tower, the four of us later took turns posing for the camera with our backs against the sea, trying to encompass as much of the blustering wind, sky, sea, and tower within our photos as we possibly could.

Up there, with the wind whipping behind my newly cut hair and the smell of the sea breeze fresh upon my nose and lips, I felt whole and safe and beautiful. It is those pictures of myself, enjoying a quick moment of peace and truly in my element—feeling truly free—that I admire the most. We all have a few favorite pictures of ourselves, don't we? This vanity was experiential and the marker of a sort of temporary revelation.

I truly liked this version of myself standing amongst strangers at the top of this windy Portuguese tower. I liked her more than I had liked myself in a long while now and I desperately didn't want her to go away.

Unfortunately, as the night filled with disagreements, I felt that version of myself slip past me.

After our disastrous dinner, the four of us went to bed in a tension-filled silence, barely speaking a word to one another.

I furiously texted Will the frustrating details of our group's fight. The way our evening had played out left it two against one, with me and Gwenyth seemingly against Alyssa, while our third friend and late arrival Alice served as a sort of shocked and innocent bystander.

I felt torn between Gwenyth and Alyssa in particular, knowing how much I depended on each of them throughout our semester abroad. I felt an uncharted loyalty to them both.

I also just felt like shit, the way that anyone does when fighting with their friends. By the time I was ready to get some sleep, a general discomfort had already settled deep within my gut.

Looking for comfort, I went to text Will goodnight as I had every other night before.

Lying in bed, I felt the culmination of every bad and lonely moment I had experienced throughout that semester bundle itself up into a package of explosives that somehow landed right at my feet. I felt dangerously close to opening that proverbial box and letting those feelings wash over me, but my exhaustion and pride refused to let me.

More than anything, I could acknowledge that it had been a shit day and that things would be alright in the morning. I was always good at reminding myself of that fact.

Really, more than anything, in that moment I just wanted a little bit of comfort from the person I loved most.

So, I texted Will: "I love you, goodnight" as I did every night.

And then I waited for his response.

By now, Will knew how difficult my night had been, and he even admitted that he wasn't really having the best day himself.

He typed back in response to my text, "Goodnight. Sleep well." No, "I love you" message back.

No, "I love you" message back.

In that moment, I admit, something inside of me broke. I opened that proverbial box of shitty feelings right the hell up and let it wash over me in waves.

I cried until it felt like I couldn't breathe.

I felt suffocated, and at the same time, so completely abandoned and alone.

Was love supposed to feel like this? Was I supposed to react like this? Did he not love me anymore?

I think, with everything from that day and that night and my feelings about the semester all jumbled up into one, it was the closest experience I ever had yet to a true panic attack.

My heart wasn't quite broken. That would of course come only a few months later. But the trust and faith I developed in Will and in our relationship now felt altered in some unfathomable sort of way.

I needed him; I needed the constancy of his love and I needed the warmth his words could provide.

I just needed that "I love you," back.

I tried to settle with what he'd given me in the hopes of finally getting some rest.

Be grateful, I told myself.

He's having a bad day too and you know that he loves you. But I couldn't rest without asking him for more, without getting to the bottom of what was going on his mind. Whatever had led to this very blatant omission, I needed to understand.

I couldn't fall asleep lying there thinking of Will, just as I had done so many months before —only this time it was for a very different reason.

I rolled over after a few minutes and sent him another text: "Why didn't you say, 'I love you' back?"

By now, the pit in my stomach started to churn, my despair congealing together with an even greater anxiety awaiting his next response.

He wrote back "I just wasn't truly feeling it in the moment, and I didn't want to say it if I didn't mean it."

I continued to lay there in the pitch black, crying to myself, trying not to wake up Alice beside me.

Maybe now my heart felt a little bit broken. Maybe now, I truly felt like a bad person—ungrateful for this trip and eager to be home, pissed off with her friends, and now somehow not enough for my partner, this man who was supposed to love me despite my flaws, but apparently did not.

Who now wasn't "feeling it," so to speak?

Submerged in my own despair, all I could do was cry. I cried myself to sleep, and as I cried, I could just about hear Alyssa's own muffled sobs out in our Airbnb's living room.

Somehow, just by the sound, I could tell that her tears weren't about our fight either. In that moment, all I wanted to do was gather my friend into a hug and simply cry together.

But I didn't.

I fell asleep in my own fit of anguish and didn't tell a single friend about that night with Will for months. I refused to reveal to anyone but him just how much he hurt me in that moment and how betrayed I felt.

There would be a few messages of reconciliation in the morning, and for now, that would be enough. But something within each of our hearts had notably changed for the worse, and our relationship would never truly be the same afterwards.

~

Later, the next afternoon, Alyssa and Alice joined me and Gwenyth as we worked our way through the gardens of Quinta da Regaleira in Sintra, Portugal. There was a stillness in the air that to me, signaled a sign of impending peace.

Things were still notably tense between the four of us, and I wondered to myself how we could clear past our qualms with one another and just be friends again.

It was Alyssa that would bring us back together.

As we each walked about the garden, admiring vibrant pink rose bushes and towering palm trees, Alyssa moved in step with me and put her arm around my shoulder.

"I'm sorry. Yesterday was just a mess and I don't like this. You've been my adventure buddy all along and I don't want that to all go away now over some stupid fight."

She took a deep breath.

"Can we be friends again?"

Standing there beside me, she chose to be the bigger and braver person than I was.

She was a better person than the one I could be in that moment.

I saw the sadness and earnestness mixed in her eyes and knew that same wistfulness was reflected back at her from my own.

"I'm sorry, too," I said.

"Of course, we're friends again. We never weren't friends— you're stuck with me."

We laughed together, and I felt an immediate appreciation for her and the sights that now surrounded us.

I later confided that I heard her crying the night before and that I hoped everything was okay. I was too scared of rejection and further conflict, too wrapped up in my own pain to be a good friend when she needed one.

Now, my friendship was entirely hers for the taking. And as I listened to Alyssa explain what was going on in her life, I felt our friendship slip back into its rightful place and move forward with its old, familiar ease.

Surrounded by the soothing flora and fauna of Sintra, our friendship got its groove back. Only, in reality, while Alyssa had opened up to me about her struggles, I had not fully opened up about mine in return. I had told her that Will and I were fighting again, but not how betrayed I felt and how my heart now ached.

I didn't tell Alyssa the full truth.

Mostly, because I wasn't ready to face the full truth myself.

Instead, I imagined myself back at the Torre de Belém, the wind whipping behind my hair and the smell of the sea breeze fresh upon my nose and lips. I thought back to the acceptance and love I had felt for myself without any restraints or reciprocated love from Will, my friends, or anyone else.

I wondered how my perspective about myself could change so rapidly within the span of one weekend. From a few quick squabbles and the devastation of a single text message.

I wondered if there was a way to find that version of myself again. I wondered if I needed to be alone to truly find her.

PART 3

CLOSURE

CHAPTER 15

GEMMA

"I'm not a baby, I'm a big girl!" I often said to my mother as a child.

"No, you're my baby—you will always be my baby," my mom would respond with a smile.

As I grew older, I would stop protesting. I would always be her baby indeed.

A few weeks after that final trip to Lisbon, I was back home, relishing in the comfort of Christmastime and a few weeks to enjoy with my mom. All the while, my mind continued to churn with possibility, along with the anxiety that now continued to plague me.

The conversation I'd shared with Will in Lisbon clouded my thoughts frequently, if not daily. I knew that I wanted to work on building and strengthening our relationship, but I wasn't sure if he really valued my efforts to become closer to him.

At times within the next few months, I would consider ending our relationship altogether, but found that I didn't have it in me. I loved him too much. Or rather, as he pulled farther and farther away from me, I loved the old idea of him so much.

I adored the person I had initially fallen in love with, but it appeared that he was long gone.

The truth was, I couldn't bear to break up with Will because I didn't want to willingly leave Gemma, my favorite of his five little sisters. Not when she reminded me so clearly of a younger version of myself.

Early on I was struck by how much seven-year-old Gemma, constantly full of attitude and spunk reminded me of me. She reminded me of my own days scraping my knees playing outside, cooking "dirt soup" in the schoolyard, and sticking my tongue out at any boy who dared sass me.

Gemma was very much of the "I'm not a baby, I'm a big girl" variety, but complete with some killer Jiu Jitsu skills. Gemma could quite legitimately kick a grown adult's ass.

Gemma was courageous, curious, and had a hilarious audacity to do and say whatever she well pleased. It was indulgent to watch her and remember that side of my younger self, and exciting to find a little young titan to genuinely believe in.

As I watched her and her dad fish the summer before, it was a joy to know that Gemma could probably keep all of the critters she caught. Her dad would be proud of every catch.

And then, when Will and I eventually did break up, he told me that the minute he had first gotten home, Gemma had immediately asked him: "Why did you break up with Liz?" in a way that seemed to imply, *you complete idiot.*

For another two months afterwards, the "Welcome Liz!" sign Gemma made for me during my first visit to Will's childhood home would continue to hang up proudly on my bedroom wall.

It was for Gemma that I kept it up for as long as I did.

Some might find it hard to believe that, but it's the God's honest truth.

My favorite professor would point out the sign once in the background while we were on a video call, and I would quickly make up some story about how it was a "sign my family had brought to the airport when I had come home from studying abroad."

I didn't want to give the awkward truth of what the sign really was, and how desperately I did not want to ever take it down.

Yet, the most important lesson I ever learned from Gemma about being a "big girl," has to do with a bracelet she gave me the month before I left for Italy, on a hot August morning, as we jumped side by side on her family's backyard trampoline.

As the sun stretched itself out over the sky above us, Gemma showed off for me—doing somersaults and flips, laughing with all of the glee a seven-year-old in the dead of summer can possibly muster. Her bright blond hair flew all over the place as she bounced and bounced, her pink tank top quickly plastered to her skin with sweat.

This time alone with her made me feel like the luckiest person in the world.

"C'mon Liz, do a flip!" she urged me.

"No, no, Gemma—you go ahead. You've got the moves going on over there! It's fun just to watch you," I said back to her.

Taking a moment to pause for a breath, I notice the small, handmade bracelet on her arm and told her:

"Gemma, I really like your bracelet. Did you make that?"

"Yeah, you can make one too if you want. Or you can just have this one."

Her eyes lit up in concentration, weighing what she's just offered. She decides quickly thereafter that I am a worthy new owner of the bracelet she made.

"Here, I'll put it on for you," she says matter-of-factly, as her compact little body stands over mine and fastens a blue bracelet with stickered flowers and hearts and butterflies around my somehow small-enough wrist.

And I say quietly, "Are you sure, Gemma? Are you sure this is for me?"

I want to give her an out, in case she's changed her mind. She is seven after all.

"Yeah of course," she says, "Now *c'mon Liz,* let's jump!"

Less than a month later, I would bring Gemma's bracelet with me to Milan for the duration of my semester abroad.

I would wear it on the plane over there and I'd wear her bracelet on the plane back home, too. I wore that bracelet and thought of Gemma every time I felt scared or lonely or unsure of myself throughout those three months so far from home.

When I wanted to be strong and be a "big girl," I would snap her bracelet around my wrist and remind myself of who I was. I'd remind myself of who I'd been—a "big girl'" like Gemma, and that even in those hardest, most terrifying moments, I could be that girl again.

CHAPTER 16

HOCKEY

———

"We would play out there," Will said, pointing in the distance. "My job was to make sure nobody did anything too stupid."

I nodded in understanding.

On the way to one of Gemma's hockey games, Will showed me where his biological father used to live, which was where he spent part of his childhood.

At times throughout our relationship, I relished the bond I thought we shared—our connection of fathers gone astray. In my head there was understanding that if we were once left behind ourselves, we would never do the same to each other.

"Is this where you had the dream?" I asked him as we still sat there in the car. Unsurprisingly, whenever we were in Will's home state of New Jersey, it was Will's job to take the "mom van" out and cart his younger siblings to hockey practice and Jiu Jitsu training and just about anywhere else.

But for these few moments, it was just us.

Months earlier, Will told me about a dream he'd had as a child where his father suddenly tried to kill him along with the rest of his younger siblings. It was a violent dream, dark and unrelenting in its nature. Will recalled waking up in terror, checking in to make sure that his younger siblings were okay.

I never forgot about that dream. In some ways, just hearing about it had haunted me too.

"Yeah, I had that dream here," he told me. Another nod, as if he were letting the memory of it sink in again.

His eyes were the tiniest bit scrunched up in the corner, as he tried to concentrate on something else. Maybe *anything* else.

I watched his jaw tense up, relax, and then tense up again.

I watched him in silence, letting him have the solitude I knew he wanted in that moment.

Will's childhood panned out very differently than mine had. After Will's father left, he was replaced—or, replaced as much as it was possible, with a stepdad that only led to more siblings and love within his family.

I had never had that father figure dream come true, and I often wondered at the beginning of our relationship if I would come to resent Will for receiving what I never did.

I can safely say now that I never did resent him for it.

As we pulled into the parking lot of a nearby ice rink to watch Gemma's game that afternoon, Will told me: "I'll never talk to my father again."

He looked at me as if to gauge my own response.

Will's face bore a fierce stubbornness that I knew all too well. Once he had made any type of decision, he was more likely than not to stick by it—no matter the cost. When he said that he'd never talk to his father again, I knew in that moment how much he meant it.

Still, I couldn't help myself.

"I think you should at least be open to talking to him," I started. "I know it's hard with the younger ones watching you, but you never know, he could try some day to be better or…"

Or he could die, like my father had and, in an instant, it would instantly be too little, too late.

I was uncomfortable vocalizing it, but there the thought was, sitting at the forefront of my mind. I didn't want to make Will feel guilty in that moment, but I consciously had to simmer my own frustration.

He doesn't know how lucky he is, I thought to myself.

He doesn't even understand how lucky he is to have the option.

Will knew me well enough to know what was racing through my mind without my having to say it.

"I know Liz, but no. This is different," he half mumbled, a faint hint of anger rising even in the hushed tone of his voice.

"I know Liz, but no," was something I felt I was hearing more and more often these days.

I finally dropped the subject and let it go.

Less than a year later, I would find myself alone again, reflecting on the relationship I'd shared with Will. In wondering about my relationship with my own father, I'd turn back to this moment and to Will's resolute anger towards his own.

I would recall the sound of his parents' minivan crunching across gravel and the biting frost of January chill. I was probably wearing the red sweater I always wore at that time, the one tucked away in my drawer still even now.

And Gemma's hockey game itself—the two of us eating sandwiches from an indoor club up above the rink and sipping hot chocolate, watching as she danced and swirled and smiled, even as she fell on the ice.

"I won't ever talk to him," seemed to echo and reverberate across the room that afternoon as we watched the girls play below us. The sternness in Will's voice clung to me like static, even as we kept score of Gemma's goals and happily chatted with Will's stepfather.

I thought back to my own decision to leave my father, and the way that he had initially left me himself. I knew that given the circumstances now, given my father's death, I would have reached out to him one last time a thousand times over. I would have tried.

Now, Will decided to leave his father behind as well, without the blink of an eye. What I didn't know at the time was that he would leave me too, only a few months after this conversation.

Maybe this comparison—or rather, paralleling —isn't fair.

Yet, as the two of us watched Gemma score another goal and high five her teammates, every memory I had of my father flashed before my eyes.

The cabin in the woods. Fishing, snickerdoodle cookies, *The Incredibles* movie.

There were so few memories, and the few that I had were so far removed with the passage of time.

"I would play out here," I thought to myself, thinking of the cold Pennsylvania woods.

"My job was to make sure my dad didn't do anything too stupid," I thought again to myself. Maybe only in retrospect could I have noticed the stench of beer that followed my father almost everywhere he went.

The cracks in my relationship with Will had made themselves clear back in Lisbon. Later conversations, like this one emphasized the distance between us. It seemed to ferment and stew into something deeper, something much more serious, something insurmountable.

The unfortunate sort of trauma bond I thought I shared with Will now appeared to be something of my own imagination. In my eyes, Will would never understand the full difference between our situations, much less the severity of his new choice.

I am with someone who gives up on people, I remember thinking to myself.

It is only a matter of time before he gives up on me, too.

I smiled again over at Will's stepfather, now a few feet away, and turned my eyes back to the game.

CHAPTER 17

N.E.D. = NO EVIDENCE OF DISEASE

———

It was the summer after Will and I had broken up, and the summer I would turn twenty-one.

I just started my new summer internship, excited for the chance to meet new people—people who could get to know me outside of my relationship with Will, and outside of all the trauma that came before it.

It was a summer of new beginnings, and final endings to come.

At this point, I was haunted by the thought of Fox Chase Cancer Center, the hospital where my mother had been treated, for years. The mere thought of hospitals in general left me stressed and uneasy. I knew the antiseptic smell and the taste of eerily preserved hospital food all too well and familiarized myself with the solitary corners hospital staff cart family members off to as often as they can.

Today, my mother would be headed to Fox Chase alone, but soon enough, the both of us would find out if her cancer was truly gone for good. It was her five-year check-up.

Her oncologists told us, with some small degree of caution, that if my mom could make it without a cancer recurrence for five years after she had initially gone into remission, she would be unlikely to go through another bout of colon cancer again.

That morning I sat alone in my childhood bedroom, conducting research on oncological services and diagnostic testing for my new job. Here I was, trying to make something so personal to me, seem professional.

Luckily, after a few early morning scans and quick tests, my mom had her results: N.E.D.

No evidence of disease.

"It went great! On my way home" is the text she'd sent me before driving home.

It went great.

"Dr. Hall said it was a less than five percent chance now that it ever comes back," my mother told me, sticking her head out the car window as she expertly backed her car into park.

But while I'm smiling on the outside, my stomach still gurgled beneath me. I wanted to celebrate in this moment with her. I wanted to email my boss and say "Hey, I know I've only been an intern here for a week, but I need the rest of the day off to celebrate right now."

It felt almost too good to be true. I urged myself to believe in it. Believe in *this*, for us.

As we rushed back into our home, smiles plastered across both of our faces, I wished I could whisper to my fifteen-year-old self.

"She's going to get better and you're going to go to college and fall in love and travel the world. She's going to get her hip replaced and retire and do swim therapy and take art classes. No matter what happens, you are both going to be okay."

I am constantly thinking of my fifteen-year-old self. Every day she seeps back into my mind—her fear, her solitude, her uncertainty.

I hoped to magically shrug away my past and this version of myself at the good news—*the cancer will likely never come back*—but she's still there beside me.

I think to myself that if I knew then what I know now, maybe the forewarning or promise of safety would have taken away the deeper bond my mother and I formed throughout this shared trauma. Maybe I wouldn't be quite the same person these five years later.

Or maybe I would have simply never known this fear in the first place.

"No evidence of disease", or N.E.D., was a term I pulled up on my phone the night before my mother made that final visit to her oncologist.

Now that definition seemed to shape our family's reality, confirmed by the doctor we entrusted with my mother's life.

Only, just a few weeks later, my mother's oncologist called her again to tell her that they wanted to do her bloodwork one more time. Run a few extra tests, just to be safe. I felt my heart catch at the thought.

I thought it was over. Did something happen?

This time, my mother asked me to come along with her.

I emailed my boss in a hurry: "I'll need the day off, I'm sorry. I need to go with my mom to a doctor's appointment."

That morning, the hours crawl by as I sit alone in the stifling summer heat, waiting for my mother's appointments to wrap up. Time seems to stop as I sit in the hospital gardens by myself, forcing myself to try to read a book, but mostly just trying to soothe my mind from imagining every worst-case scenario possible.

"How about we check out that Italian bakery nearby afterwards?" My mom promised beforehand.

"That way we can celebrate the fact that it's over."

After a short eternity of waiting, my mom appears before me—tired and slightly groggy from her bloodwork.

"Bakery?" She asks, her lips turned slightly upward to form the most careful of smiles.

"Bakery," I say back.

A short distance away, still in Northeast Philadelphia, the two of us grab Nutella *sfogliatelle* from the crochety old Italian woman that runs DeLorenzo's bakery, our latest favorite spot in the city.

Standing there, I love the woman running the shop instantly. She reminds me so much of my grandmother and of my mother beside me. In a weird way, it feels like my grandmother is almost with us. At the very least, her people are with us.

Somehow, it just feels right.

As we pay at the cash register, I let out a quick "io" before my mother interrupts me with a question. I don't remember at all what she'd asked me, but it was probably if I'd like anything else to eat before we go.

Do it again, I urge myself. Say "Io." It'll be awkward but you can do it.

I had heard the bakery owner speaking Italian herself, and I wanted her to know that I could speak it too.

"Io ho studiato a Milano per tre mese," I say in what must seem like an outburst.

I've now taken the woman aback as she turns her attention for the first time my way. She smiles at me a crooked smile, working to conceal her full grin.

"Che hai ritornato?" she asks me. I *think* this is what she asked me.

"Dicembre," I say confidently. I've been home for a while now. A part of me feels as though I never really left.

Throughout our short interaction in Italian, my mother beams with pride. This is who she raised me to be—embracing the language, the culture, the food—embracing our family, despite its deep flaws.

This is the most patient my mother has ever been, watching me speak in Italian with this semi-neighborly older woman.

After I stumble my way through a few more basic questions, my mom and I finally turn to wave goodbye and make our way out the door.

Later, as my mom gets settled into her favorite recliner that afternoon, post-*sfogliatelle* of course, she asks me to fetch her a pair of socks for her feet. Her toes must be warm if she has any chance of taking a nap.

I know she gets cold due to the neuropathy caused by her chemo and that the new sensitivity in her fingers and toes will stay with her forever.

"A pair from upstairs?" I ask her, already headed in that direction.

"No, from the car if you can. They gave me a new pair."

I feel the distinct beginnings of a smile spread across my face.

Of course, they did.

In a plain white plastic bag in the backseat of my mother's car, sits one final pair of yellow hospital socks.

CHAPTER 18

AUGUST II

——

Some six years after the death of my father, I wake up on another August morning, relishing in the stillness that now surrounds me. A soft drizzle hits the basement apartment window in the bedroom I'm staying in, but I attempt a quick morning jog anyway.

Today marks my twenty-first birthday.

I wonder to myself if August will always feel so bittersweet, this season of beginnings and endings. Celebrations of both life and death have always tended to make me feel lethargic, as a means of some sort of self-protection.

Beginnings and endings, the passage of time, the never-ending threat of change as we grow. I'm both exhilarated and terrified at the thought of it.

I think again of the morning stillness surrounding me, and wonder if it would be possible to simply hover in this type of contentment.

To simply be.

~

Throughout that August, and the months that followed, I would largely confide in my friend Ana Paula as I tried to find what type of life and what type of people might make my life feel more fulfilling. The gravity of my father's death and mother's cancer, combined with my recent breakup with Will, directly impacted the person I had become throughout the last six years, making me a more cautious and anxious person in the process.

To celebrate my twenty-first birthday, Ana Paula and I gathered with three of our close friends, drinking whiskey and eating carrot cake and laughing together for the sake of laughter itself. At this point, I hadn't laughed for the sake of laughter in a very long time.

Ana Paula and I woke up late the next morning, and by the afternoon, were in dire need of rest again.

"I think I'm going to go ahead and take a nap," she said to me later that afternoon. "My head still hurts from last night."

"Okay," I responded. "I won't be able to nap, so I'm just going to read out here."

I gestured to the sectional that sprawled across her basement apartment's living room floor. She had just moved to a new apartment, in a new part of the city, and I was there with her for a few weeks to keep her company. To keep me company too.

"You can read next to me if you want?" Ana Paula asked kindly, her soft voice rising with the question. Her eyes lit up with a smile as she pointed to the spot next to her in bed.

"Oh, that's okay, don't worry! Thank you, though," is what I replied.

I went back out to the wide beige sectional and read for about twenty minutes by myself. But then, there I felt it, a seeping feeling in my gut: I wanted my friend.

The same way I had craved the comfort of my mother, of Will, of anyone else close to me—I craved the comfort of my friend that afternoon.

And so, as Ana Paula snuggled herself beneath a weighted blanket, I sat up in bed right next to her, continuing to read Sally Rooney's *Normal People*. Reading about the precarious ups and downs of one young romance, I found solace in the unique intimacy that only close friendships can provide.

Sitting there reading, I found myself reminiscing, thinking back to the same bubble of comfort I'd felt in snuggling close to my friend Jocelyn. I thought back to the solace I'd found in my friend Lexi, who had ordered the two of us takeout Indian food that night after my breakup with Will, and in Rachel, who would send me videos to make me laugh almost daily and drop baked goods off to my mom in Pennsylvania, even if I was back in DC.

After a childhood marked by the loss of one parent—both by distance and in death, I still find myself surprised by the love I receive from those who continue to show up.

I feel marked whole and decent by their consistency and promises of later return. With time, I think I'll feel whole sitting in my own solitude.

Yet that afternoon, nestled there together with Ana Paula in the mid-August glow, I felt the weight of love, both familial and non-familial, for the first time in a very long time.

It was a kind of peace, a hovering in that solemn stillness of morning.

August had come back to life and had brought me to life along with it.

CHAPTER 19

WIND

———

There is no natural conclusion to this story, but a picture from my past draws me towards the future.

In the picture, I'm less than two years old, snuggled and buckled into my stroller, a navy hoodie keeping me warm in the brisk autumn chill.

Looking around at the world around me, my tiny hands are outstretched—reaching again and again, fingers open and shut. My eyes are a fierce blue, lit up the same way they light up now when I share something I'm passionate about with someone I trust.

"What was I reaching for?" I ask my mom, close to twenty years after the picture was taken.

"You were trying to catch the wind," she says to me with a smile.

I was trying to catch the wind.

~

No matter how much time passes, I don't think I'll ever be fully over my mother's bout with cancer or my father's absence and untimely death. In fact, I might always be jittery at the sights and smells of hospitals. I might forever feel unsettled by the thought of Fox Chase Cancer Center, where my mother was treated.

I know those halls will always haunt me, at least a little, and in acknowledging this fact, I feel just a little bit more okay.

I know that I will always feel bittersweet at the thought of my father. The fondness I feel for those early memories directly correlates with a particular twinkling in my heart. His eyes will ultimately always shine through mine.

As for Will, he'll forever remain in my past—a culmination of lessons learned.

I am happy to be in love again now.

What I can say is that I have healed, I have found my own peace and sense of self again to the degree that I'm not constantly repeating these greatest injuries, or biggest hurts, in front of my own face in the mirror every morning. Or during every second of my runs.

My five-year pity party has at last come to an end.

While, my life, my story itself, isn't quite done yet, I have nothing else insightful to share. I'm out of content. Reflections. Stories. Kaput.

I hope that more comes in the future. I wish for my life to be filled only more so with the greatest pains and sorrows and joys and tears of all kinds.

Before the end of our relationship, Will did impart one final lesson. In the throes of his own mental anguish, he relayed to me the power of the wind, a power I had harnessed so many years ago in a picture I had long forgotten, and a power that he so often lacked.

As we walked together on our college campus, Will told me:

"In the depths of everything, when I'm at my lowest, I can't feel the world around me. I don't seem to recognize my surroundings. But when I come out of it—when I come out of that lowness for a bit, the first thing I seem to notice is the wind on my face. Liz, it's like I can suddenly feel the wind again."

I never forgot that moment, the recognition of that lowness and the soft sort of power that came with beginning again. Becoming again. That was when I remembered that picture again, the picture of toddler me trying to catch the wind.

The day I stop feeling it all, the day I stop being able to feel the wind is the day that I stop living.

But in order to prevent that from happening, I'll continue to view my life in yellow, within a prism of overly embraced simple joys and the bitter lemon aftertaste of hardship.

Life in yellow is a life enriched in history and color and emotion, where my vulnerability and quickness to cry are seen as assets by those most important to me, and where that same distinctive strength only radiates back to me from them. Life in yellow is a deep breath, and a familiar feeling of warmth and love soaking through my skin, working its way from the outer edges of my being into my pores and deep down into my very bones and essence and ligaments and whatever else is in there deep inside my body.

If anything, this work is ultimately my reminder to an even older version of myself, a me in five years' time, who is taller (maybe, by then, I've fixed my posture) and brighter and still flawed and probably too neurotic but has continued to learn and grow even more.

Yet even more so, this book is a reminder to a younger version of myself, who didn't necessarily know if she could make it through the death of one parent and the health scare of another and some bouts with deeply-held anxiety and pulling oneself together and then falling so deeply and desperately in love and then feeling so alone in a country both far from home and the very essence of home and then coming back to her country only to have her heart broken and the whole world feeling like it's been set on fire.

All of that again and again and again, replaying in my mind and eventually making its way onto these pages.

But I did it, and that younger version of me did it, and I am better now because of it.

I am still just trying to catch the wind.

ACKNOWLEDGEMENTS

Most people believe that writing a book is a solitary endeavor, but I would beg to disagree. This book, as short and sweet as it is, would not be possible without a whole village of people.

To the entire team over at New Degree Press, thank you for everything you have done to support me throughout this process. Thank you to Brian Bies and Eric Koester for your leadership, and for empowering so many first-time authors such as myself.

A special thank you to my editors Katie Sigler and Katherine Mazoyer for their care in reading this book in its every iteration. Your feedback, encouragement, and enthusiasm often gave me the momentum I needed to just sit down and write.

To my undergraduate professors Dave Karpf and Peter Loge, I will be grateful for your guidance and our shared laughter always. Thank you both for always steering me in the right direction.

A big, huge thank you too to everyone who participated in my initial IndieGogo campaign to publish this book! Your support means the absolute world to me, and I wish I could give every single one of you a giant hug. Thank you to: Joy Edmondson-Irons, Shannon McGurk, Abigail Richards,

Scott Rothschild, Natalie Sites, Grace Barrett, Gwendolyn Loeber, Jesse Horowitz, Gwenyth Portillo Wightman, Julianna Gerold, Lauren Love, Megan Hickey, Babak Bahador, Timothy Clark, Lauren Belecanech, Robert Fields, Allison Herrity, Patrick O'Brien, Fiona Cahill, Taylor Kane, Rhiannon Jessell, Erik Truong, Sumriddhi Mittal, Deisha Brahma, Elizabeth Landrum, Katie Schluth, Jesse Cardinal, Erin Harden, David Karpf, Betty Hailu, Elizabeth DeCaprio, Emma Krasnopoler, Matt Rego, Alyssa Karbel, Emily Hatala, Taylor Howell, Mary Britanak, Briana Cowles, Shira Strongin, Valerie Yurk, Meredith Hessel, Andrew Parco, Emerald Wilson, Perry Warren, Rachel Yakobashvili, Jocelyn Love, Sahithi Vemula, Selin Ciesielski, Shriya Tripathi, Carlos Bautista, Allison McGurk, James Aykit, Kaitlyn Felsheim, Sabrina Veitz, Eric Koester, Olivia Dupree, Grace Montgomery, Alexandra Ghobadi, Peter Loge, Rose Risso, Stephanie Yuan, Maddie Sell, Josie Philon, Donna Kraun, Danyal Bajwa, Ana Paula Velasco, and Amber Theurer.

To my *tesoro,* I am so grateful for you. I hope this book makes you proud. I haven't shut up about it for a long time now, and I doubt I'll stop anytime soon.

To my dearest Jocelyn, thank you for sticking by me and for supporting me and my dreams through thick and thin. If there is one thing I know for sure, it is that your friendship has made me a better person. I can't wait until the day we're living in the nursing home together. I hope they make a sitcom about us.

To my grandmother, Mildred Maita Edmondson, "The Graminator," may she rest in peace.

Thank you for teaching me what it means to be tough, and how to have chutzpah. I hope you're busy making meatballs up in heaven. I'll miss watching Jeopardy and eating Pizza Hut with you always.

To my mother, *thank you*. Thank you for letting me tell our story. Every morning I am grateful because I wake up feeling your love, no matter how many miles away you are. You are the strongest and most loving person I have ever known — and everything I aspire to be. One day I will buy you your beach house, and then both of our dreams will have come true.

I love you most.

APPENDIX

CHAPTER 13

Bernard, Elyssa. "Vatican Museum Must Sees - Top 10 Things Not to Miss." *Romewise.* https://www.romewise.com/vatican-museum-must-sees.html.

Roma Citta Aperta, directed by Roberto Rossellini (1945; Italy: Minerva Film, 1946), Blu ray Disc, 1080p HD.

Made in the USA
Middletown, DE
27 September 2021